# Communication: Its Art and Soul

Printed in the United States of America

by THE ROHR JEWISH LEARNING INSTITUTE
832 Eastern Parkway, Brooklyn, NY 11213



*Cover Art:* The Conversation, *Roy Lichtenstein, 1984. Painted and patinated bronze (Roy Lichtenstein Foundation, New York)*

(888) YOUR-JLI/718-221-6900
WWW.MYJLI.COM

# Communication:

## *Its Art and Soul*

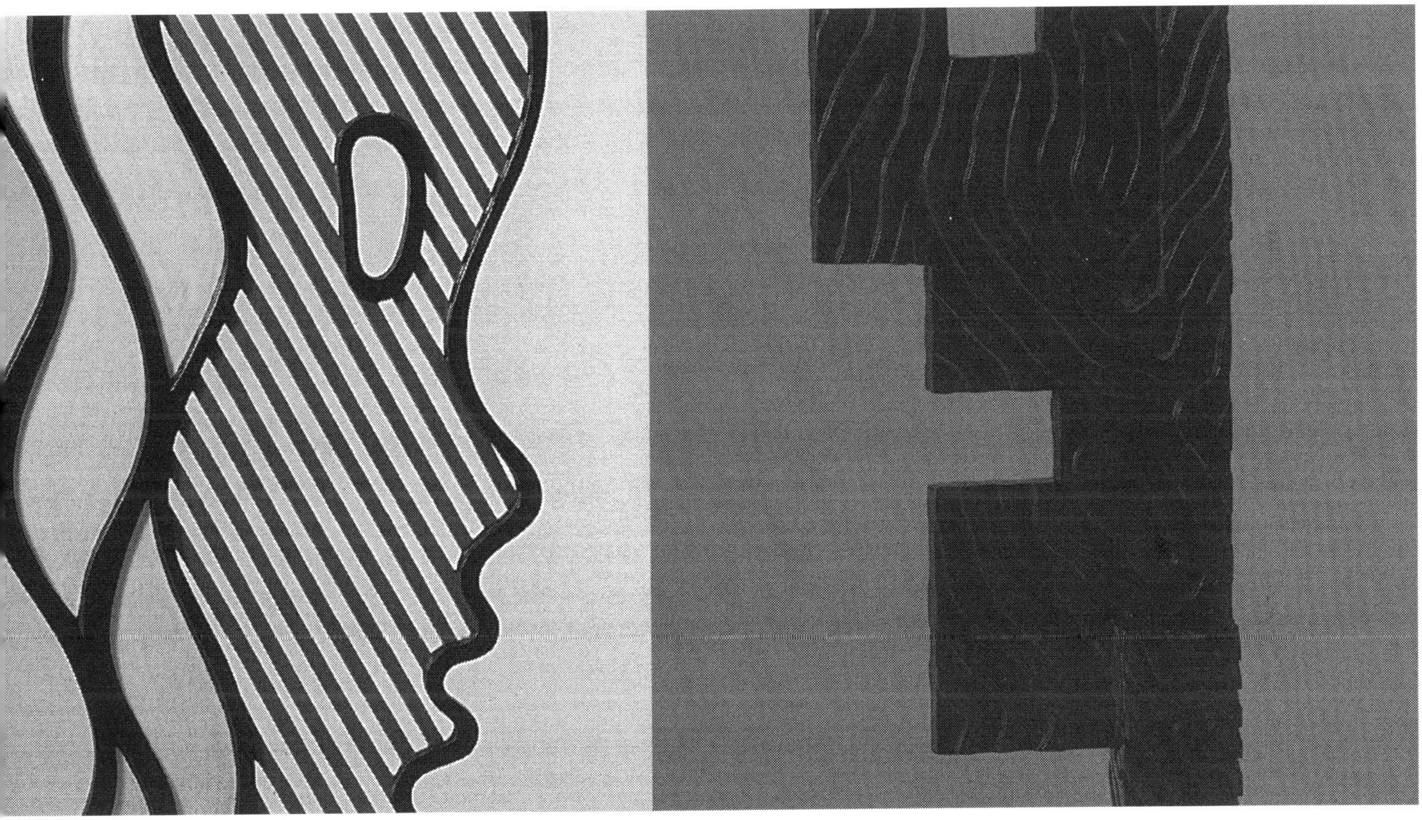

STUDENT TEXTBOOK

## ADVISORY BOARD *of* GOVERNORS

Yaakov and Karen Cohen
Potomac, MD

Yitzchok and Julie Gniwisch
Montreal, QC

Barbara Hines
Aspen, CO

Ellen Marks
S. Diego, CA

David Mintz, OBM
Tenafly, NJ

George Rohr
New York, NY

Dr. Stephen F. Serbin
Columbia, SC

Leonard A. Wien, Jr.
Miami Beach, FL

## PARTNERING FOUNDATIONS

Avi Chai Foundation

David Samuel Rock Foundation

Diamond Foundation

Estate of Elliot James Belkin

Francine Gani Charitable Fund

Goldstein Family Foundation

Harvey L. Miller Supporting Foundation

Kohelet Foundation

Kosins Family Foundation

Mayberg Foundation

Meromim Foundation

Myra Reinhard Family Foundation

Robbins Family Foundation

Ruderman Family Foundation

Schulich Foundation

William Davidson Foundation

World Zionist Organization

Yehuda and Anne Neuberger Philanthropic Fund

Zalik Foundation

## PRINCIPAL BENEFACTOR

George Rohr
New York, NY

## PILLARS *of* JEWISH LITERACY

Shaya and Sarah Boymelgreen
Miami Beach, FL

Pablo and Sara Briman
Mexico City, Mexico

Zalman and Mimi Fellig
Miami Beach, FL

Edwin and Arlene Goldstein
Cincinnati, OH

Yosef and Chana Malka Gorowitz
Redondo Beach, CA

Shloimy and Mirele Greenwald
Brooklyn, NY

Dr. Vera Koch Groszmann
S. Paulo, Brazil

Carolyn Hessel
New York, NY

Howard Jonas
Newark, NJ

David and Debra Magerman
Gladwyne, PA

Yitzchak Mirilashvili
Herzliya, Israel

David and Harriet Moldau
Longwood, FL

Ben Nash
New Jersey

Eyal and Aviva Postelnik
Marietta, GA

Clive and Zoe Rock
Irvine, CA

Michael and Fiona Scharf
Palm Beach, FL

Lee and Patti Schear
Dayton, OH

Isadore and Roberta Schoen
Fairfax, VA

Yair Shamir
Savyon, Israel

## SPONSORS

Jake Aronov
Montgomery, AL

Moshe and Rebecca Bolinsky
Long Beach, NY

Daniel and Eta Cotlar
Houston, TX

Rabbi Meyer and Leah Eichler
Brooklyn, NY

Steve and Esther Feder
Los Angeles, CA

Yoel Gabay
Brooklyn, NY

Brian and Dana Gavin
Houston, TX

Shmuel and Sharone Goodman
Chicago, IL

Adam and Elisheva Hendry
Miami, FL

Michael and Andrea Leven
Atlanta, GA

Joe and Shira Lipsey
Aspen, CO

Josef Michelashvili
Glendale, NY

Harvey Miller
Chicago, IL

Rachelle Nedow
El Paso, TX

Peter and Hazel Pflaum
Newport Beach, CA

Abraham Podolak
Princeton Junction, NJ

Dr. Ze'ev and Varda Rav-Noy
Los Angeles, CA

Zvi Ryzman
Los Angeles, CA

Larry Sifen
Virginia Beach, VA

Myrna Zisman
Cedarhurst, NY

Janice and Ivan Zuckerman
Coral Gables, FL

THE ROHR JEWISH LEARNING INSTITUTE

*gratefully acknowledges*
*the pioneering and ongoing support of*

George and Pamela Rohr

*Since its inception,*
*the Rohr JLI has been*
*a beneficiary of the vision, generosity,*
*care, and concern*
*of the Rohr family.*

*In the merit of*
*the tens of thousands of hours of Torah study*
*by JLI students worldwide,*
*may they be blessed with health,*
*Yiddishe nachas from all their loved ones,*
*and extraordinary success*
*in all their endeavors.*

Dedicated to

## Clive and Zoe Rock

and their son,

## Neil Rock

with deep appreciation for their partnership with JLI in bringing Torah study to all corners of the world.

May they go from strength to strength and enjoy good health, happiness, *nachas* from their loved ones, and success in all their endeavors לאורך ימים ושנים טובות.

In loving memory
of their son and brother

## David Rock

### דוד שמואל ע"ה בן יבלחט"א זלמן גרשון

May the study of this JLI course
by thousands of students worldwide
be a source of merit to his soul and a blessing
to his entire family.

# Endorsements

"The Rohr Jewish Learning Institute course on communication is truly artful and soulful. It covers the depth of authentic communication that the world (from a micro level to the macro level) desperately needs. From the power of listening, to the responsibility of sending messages, to working through opposing perspectives, this course will transform how you relate to all people in your life. An absolute must."

**HARVILLE HENDRIX, PHD**
**AND HELEN LAKELLY HUNT, PHD**
Cofounders, IMAGO Relationship Therapy and Safe Conversations
Coauthors, *Getting the Love You Want* and nine other titles

"In today's world of confusion and loss of direction in life, which manifests itself in young people going off into self-destructive habits, JLI is a beacon of light that can guide people to the safe haven of true happiness."

**RABBI DR. ABRAHAM J. TWERSKI, M.D.**
Medical Director Emeritus, Gateway Rehabilitation Center
Author, *Ten Steps to Being Your Best* and more than sixty other titles

"Our American culture of extreme individualism places emphasis on the self rather than the other. Some argue that our culture has caused us to lose the ability to empathize and we dehumanize those with whom we disagree. Similarly, phrases such as 'It's a free country!' and 'Just do it!' reflect the idea that we are responsible only for ourselves. This self-oriented communication is evident in both the public and private spheres. For example, various public opinion polls illustrate that communication in politics, online, and in the home has worsened during the past few years. The divorce rate for married couples in the United States hovers between 40–50% for first marriages and climbs even higher for subsequent marriages. Now, more than ever, it's important to realize our shared humanity and use communication to solve common problems in this time of extreme polarization.

"The Rohr Jewish Learning Institute's program about *Communication: Its Art and Soul* includes lessons that teach us how to be true to ourselves yet be open to the beliefs and values of others. Rather than a mere collection of communication skills, the JLI program is based on the foundation that all of us have inherent worth and dignity. Jewish wisdom, values, and ethics are the fundamental assumptions that guide each lesson, and the skills demonstrated in the course will be of benefit at home, in social settings, and in the workplace."

**SHELLEY D. LANE, PHD**
Associate Dean of Undergraduate Education, University of Texas at Dallas
Author, *Interpersonal Communication* and *Understanding Everyday Incivility: Why Are They So Rude?*

"Communication is our constant companion. How often do we stop to think about it and examine what we are giving and receiving? JLI's course on communication will suggest new ideas, refresh existing ideas, and develop skills. In-depth use of an exciting range of sources will bring participants in touch with wise ways of (for instance) dealing with social media, drawing benefit from disagreement and criticism, and maintaining confidentiality."

**KATE MIRIAM LOEWENTHAL, PHD**
Professor Emeritus, Psychology, Royal Holloway, University of London
Professor of Abnormal Psychology, New York University in London

"The Rohr Jewish Learning Institute is an exemplar of Jewish and general educational excellence. Their courses and learning materials are of the highest quality. They combine the wisdom of the biblical sages with the best in [technique]. I urge you to participate in this remarkable learning adventure."

**STEVEN HUBERMAN, PHD**

Dean, Touro College Graduate School of Social Work

"I am thrilled to show support for The Rohr Jewish Learning Institute's new course on communication. It is a wonderful endeavor. With all the electronic distractions today, we need communication skills more than ever."

**MIRIAM ADAHAN, PHD**

Author, *Sticks and Stones: When Words Are Used as Weapons, The Family Connection,* and nine other titles.

"Few behaviors are more consequential—and, at times, more counterintuitive—than communication. Because most of us communicate every day of our lives, it is easy to think we are already experts. At the same time, however, so many of us struggle to be understood and to understand others. JLI's new course, *Communication: Its Art and Soul*, helps to bridge this gap by focusing attention on the most pressing skills for social competence, including listening, managing verbal behavior, and negotiating conflict. Everyone, from amateurs to experts, can find value in these observations."

**KORY FLOYD, PHD**

Professor of Interpersonal Communication,
University of Arizona
Author, *The Loneliness Cure* and eleven other titles

"JLI presents an exciting integration of Jewish wisdom and several highly effective practices currently used in psychology. As a professional who has specialized in working with people whose life circumstances require unusual resiliency, I believe the combination of a Jewish spiritual approach along with positive psychology strategies promises to have far-reaching effects on individuals and their families. Both approaches are powerful alone in terms of enhancing well-being and together are likely to be synergistic in their impact."

**LAURA MARSHAK, PHD**

Professor of Counseling,
Indiana University of Pennsylvania
Author, *Married with Special-Needs Children*

"This JLI course on communication offers a remarkable series of teachings based on current psychological theory as well as wisdom from traditional Jewish sources. The integration of these two streams of knowledge—the secular/psychological and Jewish tradition—is remarkable. The approach is sophisticated, practical, and sure to be helpful to students who study this material. Applying the lessons from this course can help improve communication in all relationships—in couple and family life, between friends, and in work contexts. And learning the Jewish texts can enhance the spiritual as well as psychological well-being of those who attend."

**MONA D. FISHBANE, PHD**

Former Director of Couple Training,
Chicago Center for Family Health
2017 APA Family Psychologist of the Year,
Society for Couple & Family Psychology
Author, *Loving with the Brain in Mind: Neurobiology & Couple Therapy*

# *Contents*

# *Lesson* 1

## OTHERS' WORDS

### THE ART OF LISTENING

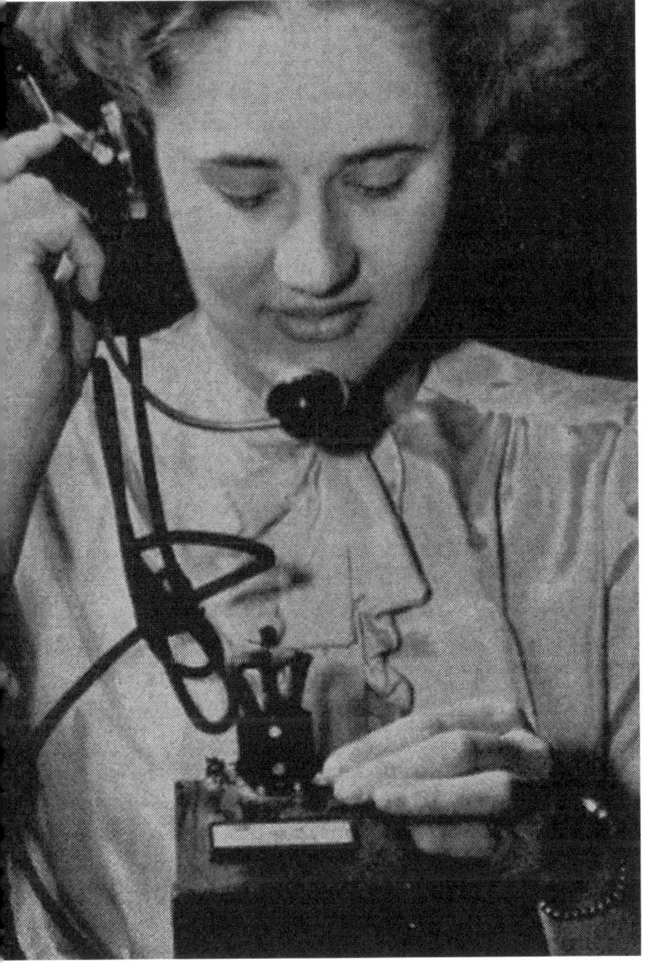

*Telephone operator,* Bell Telephone Magazine, *1922.*
*(New York, American Telephone and Telegraph Co.)*

"Most people do not listen with the intent to understand; they listen with the intent to reply."

—Stephen R. Covey

*The jaw bones begin where the ears stop. Before discovering the science of speech, it is critical to master the art of listening. Eardrums, however, are not enough; it is necessary to quiet the heart and mind to truly absorb what others have to say. The widespread difficulty in doing so accounts for a global reality that is replete with misunderstanding. This lesson turns to Talmudic wisdoms that shed remarkably relevant light on universal impediments to listening and the importance of active listening and processing.*

## Exercise 1

How many communication gaffes can you detect in the exchange depicted in the video?

| | |
|---|---|
| 1 | |
| 2 | |
| 3 | |
| 4 | |
| 5 | |

# TEXT 1

PROVERBS 18:13

מֵשִׁיב דָּבָר בְּטֶרֶם יִשְׁמָע, אִוֶּלֶת הִיא לוֹ וּכְלִמָּה.

He who responds before listening—it is folly and an embarrassment for him.

The Longshoremen's Noon *(detail), John George Brown, 1879.*

# TEXT 2

JUDITH SHERVEN, PHD, AND JAMES SNIECHOWSKI, PHD, "THERE IS A REAL DIFFERENCE BETWEEN HEARING AND LISTENING," *ISSUES I FACE* *

Hearing takes place when something disturbs the atmosphere and that disturbance takes the form of pressure waves that strike our ear drums as sound. It's the way we perceive sound.

*Listening is different. It expands on hearing when we pay attention to the meaning of what we hear.* For example, a truck just rolled by on the road in front of our house. I (Jim) heard the noisy rumble, knew what it was, and after that paid no attention whatsoever.

We do that when we're merely hearing the words someone else is speaking. They're just vibrations in the atmosphere. We nod, smile, perhaps even respond, but are we listening? Hardly. *Listening requires that we open to the meaning of the other person's words*, that we—in a very real way—enter into the experience those words are meant to convey.

It's no longer just about sound but about the thoughts, feelings, point of view, expectations, memories, sensations, beliefs—the whole of the other person—or at least as much of the whole as is available in the moment.

**JUDITH SHERVEN, PHD**
**JAMES SNIECHOWSKI, PHD**

Psychologists, authors, motivational speakers. Wife and husband duo Judith Sherven, PhD, and James Sniechowski, PhD, are practicing psychotherapists as well as corporate coaches. They have authored multiple books and speak widely on the psychology of success.

* Accessed September 28, 2017. https://issuesiface.com/magazine/there-is-a-real-difference-between-hearing-and-listening.

# Exercise 2

How Good a Listener Are You?**

*To help you become more aware of your own listening habits, complete the following questionnaire. Because we listen differently to different people, think of a specific person you have a relationship with when you answer these questions. After you finish the questionnaire, grade yourself using the scoring key on p. 8.*

When someone is talking to you, do you:

(A) Almost never (C) Often
(B) Sometimes (D) Almost always

| | | score |
|---|---|---|
| 1. Make people feel that you're interested in them and what they have to say? | | |
| 2. Think about what you want to say while others are talking? | | |
| 3. Acknowledge what the speaker says before offering your own point of view? | | |
| 4. Jump in before the other person has finished speaking? | | |
| 5. Allow people to complain without arguing with them? | | |

** This exercise is from Michael P. Nichols, PhD, *The Lost Art of Listening: How Learning to Listen Can Improve Relationships* (New York: Guilford Press, 2009), pp. 67–69.

| | | score |
|---|---|---|
| 6. Offer advice before you're asked? | | |
| 7. Concentrate on figuring out what other people are trying to say, not just respond to the words they use? | | |
| 8. Share similar experiences of your own rather than inviting the speaker to elaborate on his or her experience? | | |
| 9. Get other people to tell you a lot about themselves? | | |
| 10. Assume you know what someone is going to say before he or she is finished? | | |
| 11. Restate messages or instructions to make sure you understood correctly? | | |
| 12. Make judgments about who is worth listening to and who isn't? | | |
| 13. Make a concerted effort to focus on the speaker and understand what he or she is trying to say? | | |
| 14. Tune out when someone starts to ramble on, rather than trying to get involved and make the conversation more interesting? | | |
| 15. Accept criticism without getting defensive? | | |
| 16. Think of listening as instinctive, rather than as a skill that requires making an effort? | | |
| 17. Make an active effort to get other people to say what they think and feel about things? | | |

Key:

(A) Almost never
(B) Sometimes
(C) Often
(D) Almost always

| | | score |
|---|---|---|
| 18. Pretend to be listening when you're not? | | |
| 19. Respect what other people have to say? | | |
| 20. Feel that listening to other people complain is annoying? | | |
| 21. Make effective use of questions to invite people to say what's on their minds? | | |
| 22. Make distracting comments when other people are talking? | | |
| 23. Think other people consider you to be a good listener? | | |
| 24. Tell people you know how they feel? | | |
| 25. Don't lose your cool when somebody gets angry at you? | | |
| | Total: | |

**Scoring**

For the **odd-numbered questions**, give yourself:
4 points for each question that you answered "Almost always"
3 points for "Often"
2 points for "Sometimes"
1 point for "Almost never"

For the **even-numbered questions**, give yourself:
1 point for each question that you answered "Almost always"
2 points for "Often"
3 points for "Sometimes"
4 points for "Almost never"

Write down your score on the right-hand side of each question, then total the number of points.

| | |
|---|---|
| 85–96 | Excellent |
| 73–84 | Above average |
| 61–72 | Average |
| 49–60 | Below Average |
| 25–48 | Poor |

## QUESTION FOR DISCUSSION

Why is it difficult to listen? What are the primary impediments to listening?

# TEXT 3a

*ETHICS OF THE FATHERS* 4:1

בֶּן זוֹמָא אוֹמֵר: אֵיזֶהוּ חָכָם? הַלּוֹמֵד מִכָּל אָדָם.

Ben Zoma would say: Who is wise? One who learns from every person.

***PIRKEI AVOT***
**(ETHICS OF THE FATHERS)**

A 6-chapter work on Jewish ethics that is studied widely by Jewish communities, especially during the summer. The first 5 chapters are from the Mishnah, tractate Avot. Avot differs from the rest of the Mishnah in that it does not focus on legal subjects; it is a collection of the sages' wisdom on topics related to character development, ethics, healthy living, piety, and the study of Torah.

## QUESTION FOR DISCUSSION

Why does the wise person learn from everyone? Why should the wise person presume that a person of inferior intellect has something to teach him or her?

# TEXT 3b

RABBI DON YITSCHAK ABARBANEL, *NACHALAT AVOT*, AD LOC.

לִהְיוֹת הַחָכְמָה נִמְצֵאת בִּכְלָלוּת הָרַבִּים, וְאָמַר הַנָּבִיא, "אַל יִתְהַלֵּל חָכָם בְּחָכְמָתוֹ" (יִרְמְיָהוּ ט, כב), רוֹצֶה לוֹמַר שֶׁקְּנָאָהּ מֵעַצְמוֹ.

וְלָכֵן אָמַר בֶּן זוֹמָא, "אֵיזֶהוּ חָכָם הַלּוֹמֵד מִכָּל אָדָם", כִּי בְּהִמָּצֵא הַחָכְמוֹת וְהַיְדִיעוֹת כֻּלָּם בִּכְלָלוּת הָאֲנָשִׁים, הִנֵּה כְּשֶׁיִּלְמַד מִכָּל אָדָם יִשְׁתַּלֵּם וְיִהְיֶה חָכָם.

Wisdom is shared among the general population. The prophet said, "Let not the wise man boast of his wisdom" (JEREMIAH 9:22), for no one can claim to have gained true wisdom alone [without the contributions of others].

Ben Zoma therefore said, "Who is wise? One who learns from every person." Inasmuch as wisdom is shared by the collective of humanity, one can only gain complete wisdom through learning from every person.

**RABBI DON YITSCHAK ABARBANEL 1437–1508**

Biblical exegete and statesman. Abarbanel was born in Lisbon, Portugal, and served as a minister in the court of King Alfonso V of Portugal. After intrigues at court led to accusations against him, he fled to Spain, where he once again served as a counselor to royalty. It is claimed that Abarbanel offered King Ferdinand and Queen Isabella large sums of money for the revocation of their Edict of Expulsion of 1492, but to no avail. After the expulsion, he eventually settled in Italy where he wrote a commentary on Scripture, as well as other venerated works.

# TEXT 4

RABBI SHMUEL DE UCEDA, *MIDRASH SHMUEL, ETHICS OF THE FATHERS* 4:1

מַה מָּתוֹק מִדְּבַשׁ מַה שֶּׁמָּצִינוּ בְּדִבְרֵי רַבּוֹתֵינוּ זִכְרוֹנָם לִבְרָכָה שֶׁמְּכַנִּים אֶת הַחֲכָמִים בְּשֵׁם "תַּלְמִידֵי חֲכָמִים", לְהוֹדִיעֵנוּ הָעִנְיָן הַנִּפְלָא הַזֶּה: כִּי מֵעוֹלָם לֹא יִצְדַּק שֶׁיִּקְרָא שֵׁם חָכָם לְבַד מִבְּלִי שֶׁיִּצְטָרֵף אֵלָיו שֵׁם תַּלְמִיד. כִּי אִם אֵינוֹ חוֹשֵׁב שֶׁהוּא תַּלְמִיד, אֵינוֹ חָכָם, כִּי אִי אֶפְשָׁר לְהַפְרִיד שֵׁם חָכָם מִשֵּׁם תַּלְמִיד. וְאַף אִם שֵׁם תַּלְמִיד יִפָּרֵד מִשֵּׁם חָכָם - כִּי יֵשׁ תַּלְמִיד שֶׁאֵינוֹ חָכָם, וְהוּא בִּתְחִילַּת לִימּוּדוֹ, כִּי אָז לֹא יִצְדַּק עָלָיו שֵׁם חָכָם - עִם כָּל זֶה שֵׁם חָכָם אִי אֶפְשָׁר שֶׁיִּפָּרֵד מִשֵּׁם תַּלְמִיד.

How appropriate it is that the term that our sages use to refer to a wise scholar is *talmid chacham*, which literally translates as "a student of the wise." It is not possible to detach the word "wise" (*chacham*) from the word "student" (*talmid*), because only one who views him- or herself to be a student can be deemed wise. While it is possible to be a student without being wise—such as a student who has just begun studying and has yet to accumulate wisdom—it is impossible to be wise without being a student.

**RABBI SHMUEL DE UCEDA**
**CA. 1545–1604**

Author and kabbalist. His name, Uceda, originates from the town of that name in the archbishopric of Toledo. Rabbi Shmuel was born in Safed, where he was a pupil of the Arizal and Rabbi Chaim Vital, with whom he studied kabbalah. He grew to become a rabbi and teacher in Safed and later in Constantinople. He wrote commentaries to some biblical books, but is most noted for his *Midrash Shmuel* commentary on *Ethics of the Fathers*.

# TEXT 5

THE REBBE, RABBI MENACHEM MENDEL SCHNEERSON, *RESHIMOT* (44) 2:419–420

"כָּל מַה שֶּׁבָּרָא הַקָּדוֹשׁ בָּרוּךְ הוּא בְּעוֹלָמוֹ, לֹא בָּרָא דָבָר אֶחָד לְבַטָּלָה" (שַׁבָּת עז, ב) . . .

וְכֵן הוּא גַּם כֵּן בְּכָל **הַמְּאוֹרָעוֹת וְהַמִּקְרִים** שֶׁבָּעוֹלָם. שֶׁאֵין דָּבָר אֶחָד לְבַטָּלָה. כִּי הַכֹּל בְּהַשְׁגָּחָה פְּרָטִית . . .

וּבְתוֹר תּוֹצָאָה מִזֶּה . . . וְכָל מַה שֶּׁאֵינוֹ נוֹגֵעַ לוֹ בַּעֲבוֹדָתוֹ אֶת הַשֵּׁם יִתְבָּרֵךְ, אֵינוֹ **יוֹדֵעַ** עַל דָּבָר זֶה, **כִּי אֵין דָּבָר וִידִיעָה לְבַטָּלָה.**

The Talmud (SHABBAT 77B) states: "Of all that God created in His world, not one thing was created for naught." . . .

This principle also pertains to all events and occurrences, none of which is purposeless, for all that transpires is directed by God. . . .

A corollary of this principle is that [inasmuch as we were created to serve God,] . . . we would not be made aware of anything that is not relevant to our service of God, for no awareness or information is for naught either.

**RABBI MENACHEM MENDEL SCHNEERSON 1902–1994**

The towering Jewish leader of the 20th century, known as "the Lubavitcher Rebbe," or simply as "the Rebbe." Born in southern Ukraine, the Rebbe escaped Nazi-occupied Europe, arriving in the U.S. in June 1941. The Rebbe inspired and guided the revival of traditional Judaism after the European devastation, impacting virtually every Jewish community the world over. The Rebbe often emphasized that the performance of just one additional good deed could usher in the era of Mashiach. The Rebbe's scholarly talks and writings have been printed in more than 200 volumes.

# Figure 1.1

Listening Impediments and Tools (I)

| | LISTENING IMPEDIMENT | LISTENING TOOL |
|---|---|---|
| 1. | A lack of respect for the person with whom I am conversing | Contemplate that (a) every person has wisdom or a perspective that I lack, and (b) everything that I hear is a vital message that is intended for me. |

# TEXT 6a

NUMBERS 32:1–9

וּמִקְנֶה רַב הָיָה לִבְנֵי רְאוּבֵן וְלִבְנֵי גָד עָצוּם מְאֹד, וַיִּרְאוּ אֶת אֶרֶץ יַעְזֵר וְאֶת אֶרֶץ גִּלְעָד, וְהִנֵּה הַמָּקוֹם מְקוֹם מִקְנֶה. וַיָּבֹאוּ בְנֵי גָד וּבְנֵי רְאוּבֵן וַיֹּאמְרוּ אֶל מֹשֶׁה וְאֶל אֶלְעָזָר הַכֹּהֵן וְאֶל נְשִׂיאֵי הָעֵדָה לֵאמֹר: . . . "אִם מָצָאנוּ חֵן בְּעֵינֶיךָ, יֻתַּן אֶת הָאָרֶץ הַזֹּאת לַעֲבָדֶיךָ לַאֲחֻזָּה, אַל תַּעֲבִרֵנוּ אֶת הַיַּרְדֵּן".

וַיֹּאמֶר מֹשֶׁה לִבְנֵי גָד וְלִבְנֵי רְאוּבֵן: "הַאַחֵיכֶם יָבֹאוּ לַמִּלְחָמָה, וְאַתֶּם תֵּשְׁבוּ פֹה?

"וְלָמָּה תְנִיאוּן אֶת לֵב בְּנֵי יִשְׂרָאֵל מֵעֲבֹר אֶל הָאָרֶץ אֲשֶׁר נָתַן לָהֶם ה'? כֹּה עָשׂוּ אֲבֹתֵיכֶם בְּשָׁלְחִי אֹתָם מִקָּדֵשׁ בַּרְנֵעַ לִרְאוֹת אֶת הָאָרֶץ. וַיַּעֲלוּ עַד נַחַל אֶשְׁכּוֹל וַיִּרְאוּ אֶת הָאָרֶץ, וַיָּנִיאוּ אֶת לֵב בְּנֵי יִשְׂרָאֵל לְבִלְתִּי בֹא אֶל הָאָרֶץ אֲשֶׁר נָתַן לָהֶם ה'".

The tribes of Reuben and Gad had a great abundance of livestock, and they saw that the lands of Jazer and Gilead were ideally suited for livestock. They approached Moses, Eleazar the Priest, and the leaders of the community. . . . "If we have found favor in your eyes," they said, "let this land be given to your servants for a possession; do not take us across the Jordan River."

Moses said to the tribes of Gad and Reuben, "Shall your brothers go to war while you sit here?

"Why do you discourage the Israelites from crossing over to the land that God has given them? This is what your fathers did when I sent them from Kadesh Barne'a to explore the Land. They went up to the Eshkol Valley and saw the Land, and they [returned with a negative report and] discouraged the Israelites from crossing into the Land that God has given them."

# TEXT 6b

IBID., 32:16–18

וַיִּגְּשׁוּ אֵלָיו וַיֹּאמְרוּ: "גִּדְרֹת צֹאן נִבְנֶה לְמִקְנֵנוּ פֹּה, וְעָרִים לְטַפֵּנוּ. וַאֲנַחְנוּ נֵחָלֵץ חֻשִׁים לִפְנֵי בְּנֵי יִשְׂרָאֵל, עַד אֲשֶׁר אִם הֲבִיאֹנֻם אֶל מְקוֹמָם, וְיָשַׁב טַפֵּנוּ בְּעָרֵי הַמִּבְצָר מִפְּנֵי יֹשְׁבֵי הָאָרֶץ. לֹא נָשׁוּב אֶל בָּתֵּינוּ, עַד הִתְנַחֵל בְּנֵי יִשְׂרָאֵל אִישׁ נַחֲלָתוֹ".

The tribes of Gad and Reuven approached Moses and said: "We will build here [on the east bank of the Jordan River] pens for our livestock and cities for our children. But we will arm ourselves for battle and lead our fellow Israelites into battle until we have brought them to their place. [Meanwhile,] our children will reside in these fortified cities [for protection] from the inhabitants of the land. We shall not return to our homes [here] until each of the Israelites has taken possession of his inheritance."

# TEXT 6C

RABBI DON YITSCHAK ABARBANEL, AD LOC.

וְהִנֵּה בְּנֵי גָד וּבְנֵי רְאוּבֵן, פַּחַד קְרָאָם וּרְעָדָה מִדִּבְרֵי מֹשֶׁה רַבֵּינוּ עָלָיו הַשָּׁלוֹם. וְרָצוּ לוֹמַר לוֹ שֶׁחוּץ מִמַּעֲלַת תּוֹרָתוֹ לֹא הֵבִין כַּוָּנָתָם. כִּי הֵם בְּאָמְרָם "אַל תַּעֲבִירֵנוּ אֶת הַיַּרְדֵּן", לֹא כִּוְּנוּ שֶׁלֹּא יֵלְכוּ שָׁמָּה עִם אֲחֵיהֶם, אֶלָּא לְעִנְיַן הַיְרוּשָּׁה אָמְרוּ כֵּן, שֶׁלֹּא יַעֲבִירֵם שָׁמָּה לְהִתְנַחֵל בָּאָרֶץ.

The tribes of Gad and Reuven were terror-stricken at Moses's response. They wished to tell him that, with all due respect to his greatness, he had not understood their intention. When they said, "Do not take us across the Jordan River," they had not intended that they would not join their brothers there [in battle]. Their sole intent was with regard to their eventual inheritance; they did not wish to permanently settle across the Jordan River.

Legertocht van de twaalf stammen van Israël met het tabernakel *(The Army of the Twelve Tribes of Israel with the Tabernacle), Jan Luyken, etching, 1705. (Rijks Museum, Amsterdam)*

## Exercise 3

Think of a relationship in which you have constructed a concrete mental image of a certain person.

Can you identify times and circumstances when you habitually use that image to judge this person's words or actions?

What are alternative ways to interpret this person's words and actions?

# Figure 1.2

Listening Impediments and Tools (II)

| | LISTENING IMPEDIMENT | LISTENING TOOL |
|---|---|---|
| 1. | A lack of respect for the person with whom I am conversing | Contemplate that (a) every person has wisdom or a perspective that I lack, and (b) everything that I hear is a vital message that is intended for me. |
| 2 | Fitting what I hear into the mental image I have created of my fellow conversationalist, based on previous experiences | Clear my mind of any preexisting opinions regarding my fellow. |

## QUESTION FOR DISCUSSION

Why did the medical world reject Semmelweis's hypotheses?

## TEXT 7

TALMUD, BAVA METSI'A 85A

רַב זֵירָא, כִּי סָלִיק לְאַרְעָא דְיִשְׂרָאֵל, יָתִיב מֵאָה תַּעֲנִיתָא דְלִשְׁתַּכַּח גְמָרָא בַּבְלָאָה מִינֵיה, כִּי הֵיכִי דְלָא נִטְרְדֵיה.

When Rabbi Zeira went to the Land of Israel, he fasted one hundred days [and prayed] that he would forget the Babylonian Talmud, so that it would not impede [his ability to study the Jerusalem Talmud].

**BABYLONIAN TALMUD**

A literary work of monumental proportions that draws upon the legal, spiritual, intellectual, ethical, and historical traditions of Judaism. The 37 tractates of the Babylonian Talmud contain the teachings of the Jewish sages from the period after the destruction of the 2nd Temple through the 5th century CE. It has served as the primary vehicle for the transmission of the Oral Law and the education of Jews over the centuries; it is the entry point for all subsequent legal, ethical, and theological Jewish scholarship.

# TEXT 8

*ETHICS OF THE FATHERS 4:20*

אֱלִישָׁע בֶּן אֲבוּיָה אוֹמֵר: הַלּוֹמֵד תּוֹרָה יֶלֶד לְמָה הוּא דוֹמֶה? לִדְיוֹ כְתוּבָה עַל נְיָר חָדָשׁ. וְהַלּוֹמֵד תּוֹרָה זָקֵן לְמָה הוּא דוֹמֶה? לִדְיוֹ כְתוּבָה עַל נְיָר מָחוּק.

Elisha the son of Avuyah would say: "One who learns Torah as a child is comparable to ink inscribed on fresh paper. One who learns Torah in his or her old age is comparable to ink inscribed on erased paper."

*Cheder boys, c. 1935–1938.*
*(Photo credit: Roman Vishniac)*

# TEXT 9a

THE REBBE, RABBI MENACHEM MENDEL SCHNEERSON, *LIKUTEI SICHOT* 19:44

אִיז דֶער פִּירוּשׁ אִין "הַלּוֹמֵד תּוֹרָה **יֶלֶד**" אוֹיךְ, אַז עֶר לֶערְנְט תּוֹרָה מִיט **בִּיטוּל** (עֶר אִיז זִיךְ מַקְטִין וּמְבַטֵל ווִי אַ יֶלֶד), וָואס דַוְקָא אוֹיף דֶעם אוֹפֶן וֶוערְט תּוֹרָה **נִקְלַט** בַּיי אִים (ווִי "דְיוֹ כְתוּבָה עַל נְיָר חָדָשׁ"); אָבֶּער וֶוען דֶער לִימוּד הַתּוֹרָה אִיז **נָאר** מִיט זַיין חָכְמָה וְשֵׂכֶל (זָקֵן . . . זֶה שֶׁקָּנָה חָכְמָה), אָן בִּיטוּל, קֶען תּוֹרָה - **תּוֹרַת ה'** - בַּיי אִים נִיט נִקְלַט וֶוערְן כִּדְבָּעֵי.

The Mishnah extols the value of the Torah study of a child, comparing it to "ink written on fresh paper," as opposed to the Torah study of an elder person, which it likens to "ink written on erased paper."

On a deeper level, this *mishnah* refers not only to the Torah study of a child, one who is young in years, but also to anyone who studies Torah with *bittul.* Such a person's mind is like a child's: open to new perspectives and possibilities and therefore able to fully and properly assimilate the Torah he or she studies (in the manner of "ink written on fresh paper").

Conversely, studying Torah like an elder means to use only the tools of one's own wisdom and intellect (in Talmudic terminology, "an elder" is one who has acquired much wisdom), but without *bittul.* Such a person cannot properly grasp the Torah—*God's Torah*—that he or she studies.

# TEXT 9b

DR. YAAKOV BRAWER, "IN PURSUIT OF IGNORANCE," CHABAD.ORG

Essential ignorance is achieved when a person becomes truthfully and sincerely cognizant that he lacks understanding. In contrast to passive ignorance, essential ignorance represents a relatively advanced state of self-comprehension. In Chassidic parlance it is described by the term *bittul* (self-negation).

Essential ignorance is not a lack of awareness, but rather the awareness of a lack, and as such, it renders the mind an empty vessel prepared to receive. Without *bittul*, the mind cannot function as a true vessel to admit wisdom, because its standards of admission are distorted by bias, emotional needs, background, and habit. Essential ignorance motivates individuals to pursue truth regardless of the cost or the consequences.

**DR. YAAKOV BRAWER**
Scientist and professor. Dr. Yaakov Brawer is professor emeritus on the Faculty of Medicine at McGill University in Montreal. He lectures on neuroendocrinology and Chasidism. He has authored two books on Chasidic philosophy, *Something From Nothing* and *Eyes That See.*

# Figure 1.3

Listening Impediments and Tools (III)

| | LISTENING IMPEDIMENT | LISTENING TOOL |
|---|---|---|
| 1. | A lack of respect for the person with whom I am conversing | Contemplate that (a) every person has wisdom or a perspective that I lack, and (b) everything that I hear is a vital message that is intended for me. |
| 2 | Fitting what I hear into the mental image I have created of my fellow conversationalist, based on previous experiences | Clear my mind of any preexisting opinions regarding my fellow. |
| 3 | Superimposing the other's perspective on my own | Clear my mind of any preexisting perspective; empty my mind and focus only on the content of the conversation. |

# TEXT 10a

EXODUS 12:26

וְהָיָה כִּי יֹאמְרוּ אֲלֵיכֶם בְּנֵיכֶם: "מָה הָעֲבֹדָה הַזֹּאת לָכֶם?"

When your children say to you, "What is this service to you?"

# TEXT 10b

IBID., 13:14

וְהָיָה כִּי יִשְׁאָלְךָ בִנְךָ מָחָר לֵאמֹר: "מַה זֹּאת?"

In the future, when your child asks you, "What is this?"

The Family at the Seder, *from* The Haggadah, *Arthur Szyk, Łódź, Poland, 1935. (The Arthur Szyk Society, Burlingame, Calif.)*

# TEXT 10c

DEUTERONOMY 6:20

> כִּי יִשְׁאָלְךָ בִנְךָ מָחָר לֵאמֹר: "מָה הָעֵדֹת וְהַחֻקִּים וְהַמִּשְׁפָּטִים אֲשֶׁר צִוָּה ה' אֱלֹקֵינוּ אֶתְכֶם?"

In the future, when your child asks you, "What is [the significance of] the testimonies, the statutes, and the ordinances, which our God has commanded you?"

# TEXT 10d

PASSOVER *HAGGADAH*

> כְּנֶגֶד אַרְבָּעָה בָנִים דִּבְּרָה תוֹרָה: אֶחָד חָכָם, וְאֶחָד רָשָׁע, וְאֶחָד תָּם, וְאֶחָד שֶׁאֵינוֹ יוֹדֵעַ לִשְׁאוֹל.

The Torah speaks of four children: one is wise, one is wicked, one is simple, and one does not know to ask.

**PASSOVER HAGGADAH**

The Passover *Haggadah* was compiled during the Talmudic era. It incorporates verses from the Torah and Talmudic exegesis to tell the story of the Exodus. The *Haggadah*, which also establishes the structure of the seder, has been printed in thousands of editions and has spawned thousands of commentaries, making it one of the most popular books in the history of literature.

# Exercise 4

In the right-hand column, write the likely underlying question or statement.

| WHAT WAS SAID | WHAT WAS MEANT |
|---|---|
| Child to parent: "Why do I have to go to school?" | |
| Spouse: "Why do you have to stay at work so late?" | |
| Spouse: "Honey, would you like to stop for a drink?" | |

# Figure 1.4

Listening Impediments and Tools (IV)

| | LISTENING IMPEDIMENT | LISTENING TOOL |
|---|---|---|
| 1. | A lack of respect for the person with whom I am conversing | Contemplate that (a) every person has wisdom or a perspective that I lack, and (b) everything that I hear is a vital message that is intended for me. |
| 2 | Fitting what I hear into the mental image I have created of my fellow conversationalist, based on previous experiences | Clear my mind of any preexisting opinions regarding my fellow. |
| 3 | Superimposing the other's perspective on my own | Clear my mind of any preexisting perspective; empty my mind and focus only on the content of the conversation. |
| 4 | Listening to the question, instead of the questioner | Look for cues that inform me of metamessages. |

# TEXT 11

I KINGS 3:17–23

וַתֹּאמֶר הָאִשָּׁה הָאַחַת: "בִּי אֲדֹנִי! אֲנִי וְהָאִשָּׁה הַזֹּאת יֹשְׁבֹת בְּבַיִת אֶחָד, וָאֵלֵד עִמָּהּ בַּבָּיִת. וַיְהִי בַּיּוֹם הַשְּׁלִישִׁי לְלִדְתִּי, וַתֵּלֶד גַּם הָאִשָּׁה הַזֹּאת. וַאֲנַחְנוּ יַחְדָּו, אֵין זָר אִתָּנוּ בַּבַּיִת, זוּלָתִי שְׁתַּיִם אֲנַחְנוּ בַּבָּיִת.

"וַיָּמָת בֶּן הָאִשָּׁה הַזֹּאת לָיְלָה, אֲשֶׁר שָׁכְבָה עָלָיו. וַתָּקָם בְּתוֹךְ הַלַּיְלָה וַתִּקַּח אֶת בְּנִי מֵאֶצְלִי, וַאֲמָתְךָ יְשֵׁנָה, וַתַּשְׁכִּיבֵהוּ בְּחֵיקָהּ, וְאֶת בְּנָהּ הַמֵּת הִשְׁכִּיבָה בְחֵיקִי. וָאָקֻם בַּבֹּקֶר לְהֵינִיק אֶת בְּנִי, וְהִנֵּה מֵת. וָאֶתְבּוֹנֵן אֵלָיו בַּבֹּקֶר, וְהִנֵּה לֹא הָיָה בְנִי אֲשֶׁר יָלָדְתִּי".

וַתֹּאמֶר הָאִשָּׁה הָאַחֶרֶת: "לֹא, כִּי בְּנִי הַחַי וּבְנֵךְ הַמֵּת". וְזֹאת אֹמֶרֶת: "לֹא, כִּי בְּנֵךְ הַמֵּת וּבְנִי הֶחָי". וַתְּדַבֵּרְנָה לִפְנֵי הַמֶּלֶךְ.

וַיֹּאמֶר הַמֶּלֶךְ: "זֹאת אֹמֶרֶת, 'זֶה בְּנִי הַחַי, וּבְנֵךְ הַמֵּת'. וְזֹאת אֹמֶרֶת, 'לֹא, כִּי בְּנֵךְ הַמֵּת וּבְנִי הֶחָי'".

One woman said, "My lord, I and this woman dwell in one house; and I gave birth to a child with her in the house. On the third day after I had given birth, this woman gave birth too. We were together in the house, there was no one else present.

"This woman's son died at night, because she had lain on him. She arose in the middle of the night and, while I slept, she took my son from beside me and laid him in her bosom, and laid her dead son in my bosom. I rose in the morning to nurse my son and [saw that] he was dead, but I looked closely at him in the morning [light], and I saw that it was not my son whom I had borne."

And the second woman said, "Not so! The living child is my son, and the dead child is your son." But the first woman insisted, "Not so! The living child is my son, and the dead child is your son." Thus they argued before the king.

The king said, "This one says, 'The living child is my son, and the dead child is your son,' and the other says, 'Not so, the living child is my son, and the dead child is your son.'"

Mishpat Shlomo, *King Solomon orders that the baby be cut in half, determining the true mother, copper plate, Damascus, 1912.*

# TEXT 12

RABBI YEHOSHUA FALK HAKOHEN KATZ, *ME'IRAT EINAYIM, CHOSHEN MISHPAT* 17:15

וּסְבָרָא הִיא, כְּדֵי שֶׁיְהֵא נוֹחַ דַעַת בַּעֲלֵי דִין, וְלֹא יַעֲלֶה עַל לִבָּם שֶׁמָא הַדַיָינִים יִשְׂאוּ וְיִתְּנוּ בַּדִין וְלֹא הֵבִינוּ טַעֲנָתָן . . .

וְעוֹד, שֶׁמָא בֶּאֱמֶת הַדַיָינִים לֹא עָמְדוּ הֵיטֵב עַל דִבְרֵי טַעֲנוֹתָן, וּבְּשַׁנוֹתָן לִפְנֵי הַבַּעֲלֵי דִין יְעוֹרְרוּ אוֹתָן לוֹמַר כֹּה וָכֹה הָיוּ טַעֲנוֹתֵיהֶם.

The judges need to restate the arguments in order to put the litigants' minds at ease, so that they do not worry that the judges are deliberating the case without having properly understood their respective claims. . . .

Moreover, it is entirely possible that the judges did misunderstand the arguments. If this in fact occurred, when the judges restate the arguments, the litigants have the opportunity to correct the misunderstanding.

**RABBI YEHOSHUA FALK HAKOHEN KATZ 1555–1614**

Polish rabbi, Talmudist, and authority on Jewish law. Rabbi Falk is best known for his *Perishah* and *Derishah* commentaries on the *Arba'ah Turim*, as well as *Sefer Me'irat Enayim* on the *Code of Jewish Law*. Rabbi Falk was a pupil of Rabbi Moshe Isserles and served as head of the yeshivah in Lemberg, as well as on the Council of Four Lands, a central body of Jewish authority in Poland.

# Figure 1.5

Listening Impediments and Tools (V)

| | LISTENING IMPEDIMENT | LISTENING TOOL |
|---|---|---|
| 1. | A lack of respect for the person with whom I am conversing | Contemplate that (a) every person has wisdom or a perspective that I lack, and (b) everything that I hear is a vital message that is intended for me. |
| 2 | Fitting what I hear into the mental image I have created of my fellow conversationalist, based on previous experiences | Clear my mind of any preexisting opinions regarding my fellow. |
| 3 | Superimposing the other's perspective on my own | Clear my mind of any preexisting perspective; empty my mind and focus only on the content of the conversation. |
| 4 | Listening to the question, instead of the questioner | Look for cues that inform me of metamessages. |
| 5 | Rushing to respond | Paraphrase what I heard and attempt to clarify whether I've properly understood the speaker. |

## KEY POINTS

**1** *Hearing* is the perception of sound and the mental processing of strings of words and sentences; *listening* is opening one's mind and heart to another's words. Hearing is easy; listening is a challenging art to master.

**2** Often, it is difficult to listen because we lack respect for the person with whom we are conversing. We can overcome this difficulty by acknowledging that true wisdom is gained through communicating with people of different backgrounds, experiences, and perspectives.

**3** Moreover, every communication that we have is predestined by God and has purpose. The information conveyed to us in each of our interactions presents tools that can assist us in our life's mission.

**4** Another impediment to listening is the tendency to fit what we hear into the mental image we have created of our fellow conversationalist, based on past experiences and impressions. To truly listen, we must abandon our preconceptions about the person with whom we are communicating.

**5** Often, we are so entrenched in our own view that we cannot entertain the possibility of an alternate reality or perspective. The more knowledge we amass, the less open we are to listening to others. Humbly accepting this limitation is the very thing that overcomes it. When we are aware of our own biases, we can consciously approach information with a fresh perspective.

**6** When listening to another, we need to be on the lookout for underlying messages, and we need to always ask ourselves, *What is he or she* ***really*** *saying?* We need to resist the urge to respond to questions; instead, we need to respond to people.

**7** Before responding, we need to take a moment to reflect on what the other person has said and ensure that we accurately understood the message. It is helpful to repeat what we think we heard and await confirmation that we have accurately understood the message.

# Appendices

## TEXT 13a

NUMBERS 12:5–6

וַיֵּרֶד ה' בְּעַמּוּד עָנָן וַיַּעֲמֹד פֶּתַח הָאֹהֶל, וַיִּקְרָא אַהֲרֹן וּמִרְיָם, וַיֵּצְאוּ שְׁנֵיהֶם.
וַיֹּאמֶר: "שִׁמְעוּ נָא דְבָרָי! . . ."

God descended in a pillar of cloud and stood at the entrance of the Tabernacle. God summoned Aaron and Miriam, and they both went out [to the Tabernacle]. God said to them, "Please, listen to My words. . . ."

The Israelites' Encampment in the Wilderness, Guided by God, *J. J. Derghi, watercolor, 1866.*

# TEXT 13b

*SIFREI*, AD LOC.

רַבִּי שִׁמְעוֹן בֶּן יוֹחָאִי אוֹמֵר: מַה תַּלְמוּד לוֹמַר "שִׁמְעוּ נָא דְבָרָי"?

אֶלָּא שֶׁבִּקְשׁוּ לִיכָּנֵס לְתוֹךְ דִבְרֵי הַמָּקוֹם. אָמַר לָהֶם הַמָּקוֹם: "הַמְתִּינוּ לִי עַד שֶׁאֶדְרוֹשׁ".

קַל וָחוֹמֶר שֶׁלֹּא יְהֵא אָדָם נִכְנַס לְתוֹךְ דִבְרֵי חֲבֵירוֹ.

Rabbi Shimon ben Yochai asked: Why did God say, "Please, listen to My words"?

[Rabbi Shimon ben Yochai explained:] God said so because Aaron and Miriam wished to interrupt His words [and offer a justification for their behavior]. God therefore said, "Wait until I have concluded My words."

[If one may not interrupt God's words,] how much more so must one be careful not to interrupt the words of his or her fellow.

**_SIFREI_**

An early rabbinic Midrash on the biblical books of Numbers and Deuteronomy. *Sifrei* focuses mostly on matters of law, as opposed to narratives and moral principles. According to Maimonides, this halachic Midrash was authored by Rav, a 3rd-century Babylonian Talmudic sage.

# TEXT 14

RABBI YEHUDAH ARYEH LEIB ALTER, *SEFAT EMET, PARASHAT VA'ERA* 5659

וּבְמִדְרָשׁ (שְׁמוֹת רַבָּה ו, ה): "וְלֹא שָׁמְעוּ אֶל מֹשֶׁה" (שְׁמוֹת ו, ט), שֶׁהָיָה קָשֶׁה לָהֶם לִפְרוֹשׁ מֵעֲבוֹדָה זָרָה, כְּמוֹ שֶׁכָּתוּב (יְחֶזְקֵאל כ, ח), "אִישׁ אֶת שִׁקּוּצֵי עֵינֵיהֶם לֹא הִשְׁלִיכוּ".

וְאֵין הַפֵּירוּשׁ דַּוְוקָא עֲבוֹדָה זָרָה מַמָּשׁ, רַק עֲבוֹדָה שֶׁהִיא זָרָה לָהֶם, כִּי הַשְּׁמִיעָה צָרִיךְ לִהְיוֹת פָּנוּי מִכָּל דָּבָר.

"The Israelites did not listen to Moses's [message of redemption]" (EXODUS 6:9). The Midrash (*SHEMOT RABAH* 6:5) explains that they did not listen to Moses because they had difficulty disengaging from *avodah zarah* (idolatry), as the verse states (EZEKIEL 20:8), "[They rebelled against Me and would not consent to listen to Me;] they did not cast away the detestable things from before their eyes."

The Hebrew term for idolatry, *avodah zarah*, literally translates as "a service that is foreign." The Jews weren't necessarily engaged in actual idolatry, but in service that was foreign [to the message of redemption. This did not allow them to hear the message,] because in order to hear another, one's mind must be vacant and unoccupied [by any foreign thought].

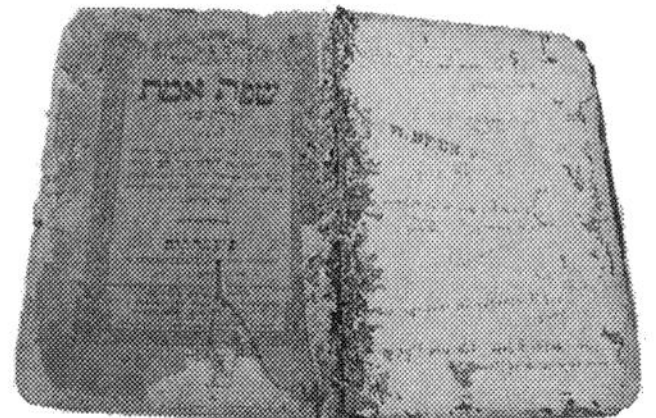

**RABBI YEHUDAH ARYEH LEIB ALTER *(SEFAT EMET)* 1847–1905**

Chasidic master and scholar. Rabbi Yehudah Aryeh Leib Alter assumed the leadership of the Chasidic dynasty of Gur (Gora), a town near Warsaw, Poland, at the age of 23. He was the grandson and successor of Rabbi Yitschak Meir of Gur, the founder of the Gur dynasty. He is commonly referred to as the *Sefat Emet,* after the title of his commentaries on the Torah and Talmud.

# TEXT 15

MAIMONIDES, *GUIDE FOR THE PERPLEXED* 1:31 (KAPACH EDITION)

שֶׁיֵּשׁ לָאָדָם בְּטִבְעוֹ אַהֲבָה לְהֶרְגֵּלוֹ וּנְטִיָּה כְּלַפָּיו, עַד שֶׁהִנְּךָ רוֹאֶה אַנְשֵׁי הַכְּפָרִים כְּפִי שֶׁהֵם מִן הַנִּוּוּל וְהֶעְדֵּר הַתַּעֲנוּגוֹת וְדַחְקוּת הַמָּזוֹן, מְתַעֲבִים אֶת הַכְּרָכִים וְאֵינָם נֶהֱנִים בְּתַעֲנוּגוֹתֵיהֶם . . .

כָּךְ יֶאֱרַע לָאָדָם בְּהַשְׁקָפוֹת אֲשֶׁר הוּרְגַּל לָהֶם וְנִתְחַנֵּךְ בָּהֶם, שֶׁהוּא מְחַבְּבָן וּמֵגֵן עֲלֵיהֶם וּמִתְרַחֵק מִזּוּלָתָן. וְגַם גּוֹרֵם זֶה מְעַוֵּור אֶת הָאָדָם מֵהַשָּׂגַת הָאֱמֶת.

We naturally like and are attracted to that to which we are accustomed. We observe this phenomenon amongst simple villagers; although they have few enjoyments and live a life of privation, they dislike city life and do not desire its pleasures. . . .

The same is the case with opinions a person is accustomed to from youth; a person tends to like them, defend them, and shun opposing views. This is one of the causes that prevents people from finding truth.

**RABBI MOSHE BEN MAIMON (MAIMONIDES, RAMBAM) 1135–1204**

Halachist, philosopher, author, and physician. Maimonides was born in Córdoba, Spain. After the conquest of Córdoba by the Almohads, he fled Spain and eventually settled in Cairo, Egypt. There, he became the leader of the Jewish community and served as court physician to the vizier of Egypt. He is most noted for authoring the *Mishneh Torah*, an encyclopedic arrangement of Jewish law, and for his philosophical work, *Guide for the Perplexed*. His rulings on Jewish law are integral to the formation of halachic consensus.

# Additional Readings

## THE IMAGO DIALOGUE – 101

BY TIM ATKINSON

**The Steps of Imago Dialogue**

Imago Dialogue is a unique three-step process for connection, developed by Harville Hendrix, PhD and Helen LaKelly Hunt, PhD. Although it looks simple, the process was formulated through extensive study of psychological theories of relationship, and clinical work with couples.

The three steps are Mirroring, Validation and Empathy, and they are described in detail below. The essence of dialogue is any conversation in which people agree to listen to others without judgment, and accept their views as equally valid as their own. We have found the Imago Dialogue to be a particularly effective way to start off on your journey to connection. You can find directions on how to use the Imago Dialogue here. What follows is a description of how to use each step.

The Imago Dialogue is initiated when a partner asks for an appointment and the other partner agrees to participate.

**1. Mirroring**

Using "I" language, one person sends a "message" to convey his/her thoughts, feelings, or experiences to the Receiver (*"I feel," "I love," "I need . . ."*). They should avoid shaming, blaming or criticizing their partner, and instead talk about themselves.

In response, the Receiver echoes the Sender's message word-for-word or by paraphrasing, using a lead sentence like, *"Let me see if I've got you. You said . . . "*

Mirroring helps me to listen to what the other person is actually saying rather than listening to the reactions and responses going on in my head while my partner is talking.

Then there's a beautiful question the receiver can ask: *"Is there more?"* When I ask that question I leave a little time, to show I really mean it, and want to hear more. Often my partner might pause *"Well no . . . er, let me see . . . maybe there is."* Often as they are given space and time, they will go deeper and share more with me, and that sharing can be the most fascinating part.

Keep on with it. You might be more encouraging: *"Wow. Interesting. Is there more about that?"* The more I reassure my partner that I am open to what she is saying, the more I can voyage on a wonderful journey into her world, and experience connection, even if I do find the subject area challenging or unfamiliar.

When my partner says, *"No, that's all,"* then I can try a summary. *"So, in summary I heard you say that . . . ."* Then check that you got it all. My partner might often say, *"Well you missed this little bit—and it's quite important to me that you hear it."*

**2. Validation**

When I mirror my partner well, they will probably already be feeling that I have heard their point of view, and seen that for them it is valid. But it's nice to say that too.

This part of the process can be quite hard too, if my partner has a very different perspective on things from mine. But to be connected, it's important for me to recognize that what my partner says makes sense for her. Sometimes her view might be so different from mine that I am tempted to think that she must be wrong. But in dialogue, creating the connection is paramount. Who is right and who is wrong doesn't matter. Harville Hendrix likes to say: ***"You can be right, or you can be married!"*** With this process,

**TIM ATKINSON**

Tim Atkinson is executive director of Imago Relationships International. Imago provides couples therapy and couples workshops around the world.

you might even discover that you can find a solution together where it doesn't matter whether either of you are right or wrong over this issue, because the underlying pain is what really needs to be addressed. Precisely because you are in relationship with another person, it is healthy to be able to accept that you hold different viewpoints.

After I have summarized my partner, I can validate them by simply saying, *"That makes sense to me."* I don't have to agree with her, but show that I respect her reality. If I can, I might go on: *"That makes sense to me because . . ."*

Sometimes as I watch my partner when I see this, I can see a physical sign of relief. It's a lovely thing to have your views validated by another.

**3. Empathy**

The third and final step of the Imago Dialogue is empathy. In the empathy step, I imagine what my partner might be feeling. Feelings are simple words like "Angry, Sad, Lonely, Afraid, Happy, Joyful, etc."

I would just ask my partner, *"I imagine you might be feeling afraid, and perhaps a little sad too. Is that what you are feeling?"* Then I check in with my partner, and if she shares other feelings, then I mirror them to show I heard. *"Ah, a little excited, too."*

Did you try that with your partner? How do you feel? Did it help you understand them a little more, and bring you closer? I hope so. It has made a huge difference in my life.

**Directions for a Simple Imago Dialogue**

You can begin to use the Imago Dialogue to share with your partner something that concerns you, and that you would like to share with them. A great way to start using the dialogue is to share something that you appreciate about your partner. Try it, and see how you feel when your partner mirrors back your appreciation of them.

Here are some specific phrases you can use as you practice dialogue

**Sender**

*I would like to dialogue about . . .*
*Is now okay?*
*I feel . . .*
*I love . . .*
*I need . . .*
*What's bothering me is . . .*

**Receiver**

1. Mirroring
*Let me see if I've got you.*
*I heard you say . . . or You said . . .*
*Am I getting you? Or: Did I get that?*
*Is there more about that?*
*Summary mirror*
*Let me see if I got it all. . . .?*
*Am I getting you? Did I get all of that?*
*Or: Is that a good summary?*
2. Validation
*You make sense to me, and what makes sense is . . .*
*I can understand that . . . given that . . .*
*I can see how you would see it that way because sometimes I do . . .*
3. Empathy
*I imagine you might be feeling . . .*
*Is that what you're feeling?*

**Switch Roles**

# BECOME A BETTER LISTENER: ACTIVE LISTENING

BY JOHN M. GROHOL, PSY.D.

We all go through our daily lives engaging in many conversations with friends, co-workers, and our family members. But most of the time, we don't listen as well as we could or sometimes should. We're often distracted by other things in the environment, such as the television, the Internet, our cell phones, or something else. We think we're listening to the other person, but we're really not giving them our full attention.

Enter a skill called "active listening." Active listening is all about building rapport, understanding, and trust. By learning the skills below, you will become a better listener and *actually hear* what the other person is saying—not just what you think they are saying or what you want to hear. While therapists are often made fun of for engaging in active listening, it is a proven psychological technique that helps people talk. It also helps a person feel free to continue talking even if the person they are talking to doesn't have a lot to offer the other person (other than their ear).

Are you as good a listener as you think you are?

**Thirteen Steps to Better Active Listening Skills**

Below you will find 13 different skills that help people be better active listeners. You do not have to become adept at each of these skills to be a good active listener, but the more you do, the better you'll be. If you even just use 3 or 4 of these skills, you will find yourself listening and hearing more of what another person is saying to you.

1. *Restating*: To show you are listening, repeat every so often what you think the person said—not by parroting, but by paraphrasing what you heard in your own words. For example, "Let's see if I'm clear about this. . . ."
2. *Summarizing:* Bring together the facts and pieces of the problem to check understanding—for example, "So it sounds to me as if . . ." Or, "Is that it?"
3. *Minimal encouragers:* Use brief, positive prompts to keep the conversation going and show you are listening—for example, "umm-hmmm," "Oh?" "I understand," "Then?" "And?"
4. *Reflecting:* Instead of just repeating, reflect the speaker's words in terms of feelings—for example, "This seems really important to you. . . ."
5. *Giving feedback:* Let the person know what your initial thoughts are on the situation. Share pertinent information, observations, insights, and experiences. Then listen carefully to confirm.
6. *Emotion labeling:* Putting feelings into words will often help a person to see things more objectively. To help the person begin, use "door openers"—for example, "I'm sensing that you're feeling frustrated . . . worried . . . anxious . . ."
7. *Probing:* Ask questions to draw the person out and get deeper and more meaningful information—for example, "What do you think would happen if you . . .?"
8. *Validation:* Acknowledge the individual's problems, issues, and feelings. Listen openly and with empathy, and respond in an interested way—for example, "I appreciate your willingness to talk about such a difficult issue. . . ."
9. *Effective pause:* Deliberately pause at key points for emphasis. This will tell the person you are saying something that is very important to them.
10. *Silence:* Allow for comfortable silences to slow down the exchange. Give a person time to think as well as talk. Silence can also be very helpful in diffusing an unproductive interaction.
11. *"I" messages:* By using "I" in your statements, you focus on the problem not the person. An I-message lets the person know what you feel and

**JOHN M. GROHOL, PSY.D**

John M. Grohol is a mental health and human behavior expert, published researcher, author, and creator and CEO of the mental health and psychology network, *Psychcentral.com.*

why—for example, "I know you have a lot to say, but I need to . . ."

12. *Redirecting:* If someone is showing signs of being overly aggressive, agitated, or angry, this is the time to shift the discussion to another topic.
13. *Consequences:* Part of the feedback may involve talking about the possible consequences of inaction. Take your cues from what the person is saying—for example, "What happened the last time you stopped taking the medicine your doctor prescribed?"

**Seven Communication Blockers**

These roadblocks to communication can stop communication dead in its tracks:

1. "Why" questions. They tend to make people defensive.
2. Quick reassurance, saying things like, "Don't worry about that."
3. Advising—"I think the best thing for you is to move to assisted living."
4. Digging for information and forcing someone to talk about something they would rather not talk about.
5. Patronizing—"You poor thing, I know just how you feel."
6. Preaching—"You should . . ." Or, "You shouldn't . . ."
7. Interrupting—Shows you aren't interested in what someone is saying.

**Five Simple Conversation Courtesies**

1. "Excuse me . . ."
2. "Pardon me . . ."
3. "One moment please . . ."
4. "Let's talk about solutions."
5. "May I suggest something?"

**The Art of Questioning**

The four main types of questions are:

1. *Leading Questions:* For example, "Would you like to talk about it?" "What happened then?" Could you tell me more?"
2. *Open-ended Questions:* Use open-ended questions to expand the discussion—for example, lead with: "How? What? Where? Who? Which?"
3. *Closed-ended Questions:* Use closed ended questions to prompt for specifics—for example, lead with: "Is? Are? Do? Did? Can? Could? Would?"
4. *Reflective Questions:* Can help people understand more about what they said—for example, someone tells you, "I'm worried I won't remember. . . ." Reflective Q: "It sounds like you would like some help remembering?"

National Aging Information & Referral Support Center

# NOTHING REALLY MATTERS:
## A "MOMENT OF SILENCE" TO START THE SCHOOL DAY

BY RABBI YISRAEL RICE

Have I complained before about life moving too quickly? (Or am I just getting old?) Today, I would like to complain about .5 of a second. It happened so quickly, but it continues to disturb me. Actually, what did not happen is what's bothering me. And what did not happen? Well, nothing is what did not happen, and it did not happen at a point when I really needed nothing.

Are you familiar with that .5 seconds of "nothing" of which I speak? It is the pause in a conversation that gives you the feeling that something meaningful is happening. It implies that the other person is actually listening and absorbing what you had to say. And then comes a thoughtful response. It is a mere half a second, but this little "nothing" carries profound meaning.

That pause in a conversation is just as important as the words that follow it. It may even be more essential. Look at the white spaces between the letters on this page; aren't they as important as the letters themselves? The pause in music can convey an even more powerful message than the chords. Silence gives significance to that which is around it.

The Talmud (Megillah 18) tells us that if a word is worth a *selah* (the currency of that time), silence is worth two. With all the information and noise flying around in our day, I think the silence premium may have even risen.

There is one very practical and beneficial way to apply this silence. By beneficial, I mean that it could elevate the entire platform of our society.Each and every school day, tens of millions of children begin their day of study and growth. They jump right into their invigorating subjects of arithmetic, social studies, science, English, etc. But what does it all *mean*? What purpose does it serve? What will they do with all this knowledge and expertise five, ten and 50 years down the road? Will they use it to benefit themselves, their fellow human beings and the world in which they live? Or, will they make this world a little less livable?

In the history of mankind—including its fairly recent history—there have been societies that excelled in academics but failed miserably when it came to humanity. According to many recent studies, even in our own society nothing really matters. We are raising a generation of entitlement with flimsy moral values (a slight overstatement).

Perhaps what we need is a little "white space." A moment of silence.

We can empower our children with "nothing." A moment at the beginning of their day that could give context and meaning to the hours that follow. During this moment, the children could reflect on meaning—on the *why* of their learning, rather than just the how.

The obvious question, of course, is: who would give them that meaning? Two hundred years ago, we Americans decided that we don't want a state religion. We don't want the government dispensing moral guidance to our children. That's why we have the "Establishment Clause" in our Constitution mandating the separation of church and state. Rightly or wrongly, this means that no public school teacher can get up in front of the classroom and speak about a moral code of conduct predicated upon man's responsibility to a Higher Authority.

That's why we need a moment of silence. The only instruction public school children will get from their teachers is that they should utilize this time for personal reflection. And who will tell them what to think about? What a great question! How about their

**RABBI YISRAEL RICE**

Rabbi Yisrael Rice is the executive director of Chabad of Marin, in Marin County, California, where he has led and educated the community for more than 30 years. He is the author of *SoulQuest* and *The Kabbalah of Now*, and he serves as the chairman of the editorial board of the Jewish Learning Institute.

parents? This could bring about a phenomenal unintended consequence: a dialogue between children and parents about meaning.

For those parents who choose to do so, this will be an opportunity to talk with their children about a Creator Who bestows life and to Whom we are accountable. And for all parents, it will be a means of connecting their children's academic studies to the moral values they wish to pass on to them.

In this way, space can be made in the consciousness of our children for a higher purpose for their learning. Worst case scenario is they will daydream about the same thing they dream about during history class. Nothing lost. The best case scenario is our next generation will start their day with a focus on something higher. All of their subjects of study, and indeed their entire life, will be given context and meaning. Nothing really matters.

Chabad.org
Reprinted with permission of the publisher

## THE SOUND OF SILENCE

BY RABBI LORD JONATHAN SACKS

Bamidbar is usually read on the Shabbat before Shavuot. So the sages connected the two. Shavuot is the time of the giving of the Torah. Bamidbar means "in the desert." What then is the connection between the desert and the Torah, the wilderness and God's word?

The sages gave several interpretations. According to the Mechilta the Torah was given publicly, openly, and in a place no one owns because had it been given in the land of Israel, Jews would have said to the nations of the world, "You have no share in it." Instead, whoever wants to come and accept it, let them come and accept it.[1]

Another explanation: Had the Torah been given in Israel the nations of the world would have had an excuse for not accepting it. This follows the rabbinic tradition that before God gave the Torah to the Israelites He offered it to all the other nations, and each found a reason to decline.[2]

Yet another: Just as the wilderness is free—it costs nothing to enter—so the Torah is free. It is God's gift to us.[3]

But there is another, more spiritual reason. The desert is a place of silence. There is nothing visually to distract you, and there is no ambient noise to muffle sound. To be sure, when the Israelites received the Torah, there was thunder and lightning and the sound of a shofar. The earth felt as if it were shaking at its foundations. But in a later age, when the prophet Elijah stood at the same mountain after his confrontation with the prophets of Baal, he encountered God not in the whirlwind or the fire or the earthquake, but in the *kol demamah dakah*, the still, small voice, literally "the sound of a slender silence."[4] I define this as *the sound you can only hear if you are listening*. In the silence of the *midbar*, the desert, you can hear the *Medaber*, the Speaker, and the *medubar*, that which is spoken. To hear the voice of God you need a listening silence in the soul.

**RABBI LORD JONATHAN SACKS, PHD, 1948–**

Former chief rabbi of the United Kingdom. Rabbi Sacks attended Cambridge University and received his doctorate from King's College, London. A prolific and influential author, his books include *Will We Have Jewish Grandchildren?* and *The Dignity of Difference*. He received the Jerusalem Prize in 1995 for his contributions to enhancing Jewish life in the Diaspora, was knighted and made a life peer in 2005, and became Baron Sacks of Aldridge in 2009.

Many years ago British television produced a documentary series, *The Long Search*, on the world's great religions.[5] When it came to Judaism, the presenter Ronald Eyre seemed surprised by its blooming, buzzing confusion, especially the loud, argumentative voices in the Beit Midrash, the house of study. Remarking on this to Elie Wiesel, he asked, "Is there such a thing as a *silence* in Judaism?" Wiesel replied, "Judaism is full of silences . . . but *we don't talk about them*."

Judaism is a very verbal culture, a religion of holy words. Through words, God created the universe: "And God said, 'Let there be' . . . and there was." According to the Targum, it is our ability to speak that makes us human. It translates the phrase "and man became a living soul" (Gen. 2:7) as "and man became a *speaking* soul." Words create. Words communicate. Our relationships are shaped, for good or bad, by language. Much of Judaism is about the power of words to make or break worlds.

So silence in Tanach often has a negative connotation. "Aaron was silent," says the Torah, after the death of his two sons Nadav and Avihu (Lev. 10:3). "The dead do not praise You," says Psalm 115, "nor do those who go down to the silence [of the grave]." When Job's friends came to comfort him after the loss of his children and other afflictions, "Then they sat down with him on the ground for seven days and seven nights, yet no one spoke a word to him, for they saw that his pain was very great" (Job 2:13).

But not all silence is sad. Psalms tells us that "to You, silence is praise" (Ps. 65:2). If we are truly in awe at the greatness of God, the vastness of the universe, and the almost infinite extent of time, our deepest emotions will indeed lie too deep for words. We will experience silent communion.

The sages valued silence. They called it "a fence to wisdom."[6] If words are worth a coin, silence is worth two.[7] Raban Shimon ben Gamliel said, "All my days I have grown up among the wise, and I have found nothing better than silence."[8]

The service of the priests in the Temple was accompanied by silence. The Levites sang in the courtyard, but the priests—unlike their counterparts in other ancient religions—neither sang nor spoke while offering the sacrifices. One scholar[9] has accordingly spoken of "the silence of the sanctuary." The Zohar (2a) speaks of silence as the medium in which both the Sanctuary above and the Sanctuary below are made.

There were Jews who cultivated silence as a spiritual discipline. Bratslav Hassidim meditate in the fields. There are Jews who practise *taanit dibbur*, a "fast of words." Our most profound prayer, the private saying of the *Amidah*, is called *tefillah be-lachash*, the "silent prayer." It is based on the precedent of Hannah, praying for a child: "She spoke in her heart. Her lips moved but her voice was not heard" (1 Sam. 1:13).

God hears our silent cry. In the agonising tale of how Sarah told Abraham to send Hagar and her son away, the Torah tells us that when their water ran out and the young Ishmael was at the point of dying, Hagar cried, yet God heard "the voice of the child" (Gen. 21:16-17). Earlier, when the angels came to visit Abraham and told him that Sarah would have a child, Sarah laughed inwardly, that is, silently, yet she was heard by God (Gen. 18:12-13). God hears our thoughts even when they are not expressed in speech.

The silence that counts, in Judaism, is thus a listening silence—and listening is the supreme religious art. Listening means making space for others to speak and be heard. As I point out in my commentary to the Siddur, there is no English word that remotely equals the Hebrew verb *sh-m-a* in its wide range of senses: to listen, to hear, to pay attention, to understand, to internalise and to respond in deed.

This was one of the key elements in the Sinai covenant, when the Israelites, having already said twice, "All that God says, we will do," then said, "All that God says, we will do and we will hear [*venishma*]" (Ex. 24:7). It is the *nishma*—listening, hearing, heeding, responding—that is the key religious act.

Thus, Judaism is not only a religion of doing and speaking; it is also a religion of listening. Faith is *the ability to hear the music beneath the noise*. There is the silent music of the spheres, about which Psalm 19 speaks:

*The heavens declare the glory of God*
*The skies proclaim the work of His hands.*
*Day to day they pour forth speech,*
*Night to night they communicate knowledge.*
*There is no speech, there are no words,*

*Their voice is not heard.*
*Yet their music carries throughout the earth.*

There is the voice of history that was heard by the prophets. And there is the commanding voice of Sinai, that continues to speak to us across the abyss of time. I sometimes think that people in the modern age have found the concept of "Torah from heaven" problematic, not because of some new archaeological discovery, but because we have lost the habit of listening to the sound of transcendence, a voice beyond the merely human.

It is fascinating that despite his often fractured relationship with Judaism, Sigmund Freud created in psychoanalysis a deeply Jewish form of healing. He himself called it the "speaking cure," but it is in fact a *listening* cure. Almost all effective forms of psychotherapy involve deep listening.

Is there enough listening in the Jewish world today? Do we, in marriage, really listen to our spouses? Do we as parents truly listen to our children? Do we, as leaders, hear the unspoken fears of those we seek to lead? Do we internalise the sense of hurt of the people who feel excluded from the community? Can we really claim to be listening to the voice of God if we fail to listen to the voices of our fellow humans?

In his poem "In Memory of W. B. Yeats," W. H. Auden wrote:

*In the deserts of the heart*
*Let the healing fountain start.*

From time to time we need to step back from the noise and hubbub of the social world and create in our hearts the stillness of the desert where, within the silence, we can hear the *kol demamah dakah*, the still, small voice of God, telling us we are loved, we are heard, we are embraced by God's everlasting arms, we are not alone.

Rabbisacks.org
Reprinted with permission of the author

**Endotes**

1 Mechilta, Yitro, *Bachodesh*, 1.
2 Ibid., 5.
3 Ibid.
4 1 Kings 19:9-12.
5 BBC television, first shown 1977.
6 Avot 3:13.
7 Megilah 18a.
8 Avot 1:17.
9 Israel Knohl.

# *Lesson* 2

# WISE WORDS

## THE ART OF POSITIVE COMMUNICATION

Scholars at a Lecture, *William Hogarth, 1736. (National Gallery of Art, Washington, D.C.)*

"Wise men speak because they have something to say; fools speak because they have to say something."

—Plato

*In today's age of social media, the borders of privacy have grown befuddled. In a world where all is bared and none is barred, it is difficult to strike the right balance. This lesson draws on the Torah's insights into the everyday dilemmas of when to broach an opinion and when to keep silent, what to share and what to retain—and how to use words in the most powerful way.*

# Exercise 1

How many communication gaffes can you detect in the exchange depicted in the video?

| | |
|---|---|
| 1 | |
| 2 | |
| 3 | |
| 4 | |
| 5 | |

# TEXT 1a

*ETHICS OF THE FATHERS* 1:17

שִׁמְעוֹן בְּנוֹ אוֹמֵר, "כָּל יָמַי גָּדַלְתִּי בֵּין הַחֲכָמִים, וְלֹא מָצָאתִי לַגּוּף טוֹב מִשְּׁתִיקָה".

Shimon, the son [of Rabban Gamliel], would say: "All my life I was raised among the wise, and I have found nothing to be more beneficial for the body than silence."

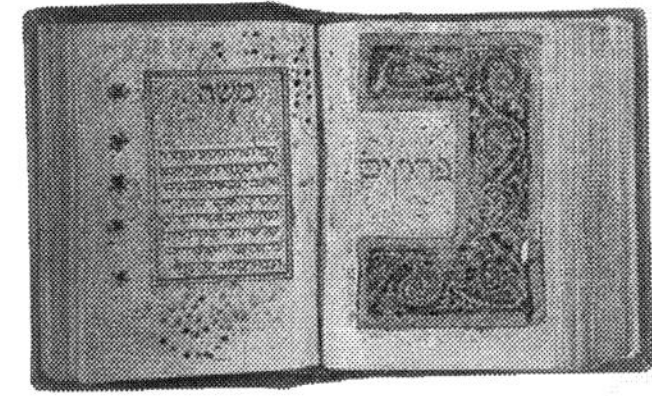

***PIRKEI AVOT***
**(ETHICS OF THE FATHERS)**

A 6-chapter work on Jewish ethics that is studied widely by Jewish communities, especially during the summer. The first 5 chapters are from the Mishnah, tractate Avot. Avot differs from the rest of the Mishnah in that it does not focus on legal subjects; it is a collection of the sages' wisdom on topics related to character development, ethics, healthy living, piety, and the study of Torah.

# TEXT 1b

TALMUD, MEGILAH 18A

כִּי אָתָא רַב דִּימִי, אָמַר:
אָמְרֵי בְּמַעֲרָבָא: "מִלָּה בְּסֶלַע, מַשְׁתּוּקָא בִּתְרֵין".

When Rabbi Dimi arrived [in Babylonia] he related:

In the West [i.e., the Land of Israel] they say: "If a word is worth one coin, silence is worth two."

**BABYLONIAN TALMUD**

A literary work of monumental proportions that draws upon the legal, spiritual, intellectual, ethical, and historical traditions of Judaism. The 37 tractates of the Babylonian Talmud contain the teachings of the Jewish sages from the period after the destruction of the 2nd Temple through the 5th century CE. It has served as the primary vehicle for the transmission of the Oral Law and the education of Jews over the centuries; it is the entry point for all subsequent legal, ethical, and theological Jewish scholarship.

# Exercise 2

Why is silence a virtue? List as many reasons as come to mind.

| | |
|---|---|
| 1 | |
| 2 | |
| 3 | |
| 4 | |

# TEXT 2

TALMUD, YOMA 72B

זָכָה, נַעֲשֵׂית לוֹ סַם חַיִים. לֹא זָכָה, נַעֲשֵׂית לוֹ סַם מִיתָה.

If one is worthy, Torah study is a potion of life. If one is unworthy, Torah study is a potion of death.

Rabbi, *Max Weber, 1940. (The Phillips Collection)*

# TEXT 3

*ETHICS OF THE FATHERS* 5:7

> שִׁבְעָה דְבָרִים בְּגוֹלֶם וְשִׁבְעָה בְּחָכָם.
>
> חָכָם: אֵינוֹ מְדַבֵּר לִפְנֵי מִי שֶׁגָּדוֹל מִמֶּנּוּ בְּחָכְמָה וּבְמִנְיָן,
> וְאֵינוֹ נִכְנָס לְתוֹךְ דִּבְרֵי חֲבֵרוֹ,
> וְאֵינוֹ נִבְהָל לְהָשִׁיב,
> שׁוֹאֵל כְּעִנְיָן וּמֵשִׁיב כַּהֲלָכָה,
> וְאוֹמֵר עַל רִאשׁוֹן רִאשׁוֹן וְעַל אַחֲרוֹן אַחֲרוֹן,
> וְעַל מַה שֶּׁלֹּא שָׁמַע, אוֹמֵר "לֹא שָׁמַעְתִּי",
> וּמוֹדֶה עַל הָאֱמֶת.
>
> וְחִלּוּפֵיהֶן בְּגוֹלֶם.

There are seven characteristic features that are found in a *golem* (foolish person) and seven in a wise person.

Wise people:

1. do not speak in front of one who is greater than they in wisdom and in age;
2. do not interrupt the words of another;
3. do not respond impulsively;
4. ask to the point and answer as is proper;
5. respond to the first point first and to the last point last;
6. [when discussing a topic] in which they are not versed, they say, "I have not heard";
7. concede to the truth.

The opposites of these traits are found in the *golem*.

## QUESTION FOR DISCUSSION

What *actionable* messages does this *mishnah* convey?

## TEXT 4

MISHNAH, PE'AH 8:9

> וְכָל מִי שֶׁאֵינוֹ צָרִיךְ לִטֹּל וְנוֹטֵל, אֵינוֹ נִפְטָר מִן הָעוֹלָם עַד שֶׁיִּצְטָרֵךְ לַבְּרִיּוֹת. וְכָל מִי שֶׁצָּרִיךְ לִטֹּל וְאֵינוֹ נוֹטֵל, אֵינוֹ מֵת מִן הַזִּקְנָה, עַד שֶׁיְּפַרְנֵס אֲחֵרִים מִשֶּׁלּוֹ . . .
>
> וְכָל מִי שֶׁאֵינוֹ לֹא חִגֵּר, וְלֹא סוּמָא, וְלֹא פִסֵּחַ, וְעוֹשֶׂה עַצְמוֹ כְּאַחַד מֵהֶם, אֵינוֹ מֵת מִן הַזִּקְנָה עַד שֶׁיִּהְיֶה כְּאַחַד מֵהֶם.

Whoever does not need to take [charity] and yet takes, will not die before actually needing financial assistance. [Conversely,] one who requires financial assistance and yet does not avail himself of charity, will not die of old age before supporting others from his own [bounty]. . . .

One who feigns lameness, blindness, or impaired mobility will not die of old age before he actually becomes like one of these.

**MISHNAH**

The first authoritative work of Jewish law that was codified in writing. The Mishnah contains the oral traditions that were passed down from teacher to student; it supplements, clarifies, and systematizes the commandments of the Torah. Due to the continual persecution of the Jewish people, it became increasingly difficult to guarantee that these traditions would not be forgotten. Rabbi Yehudah Hanasi therefore redacted the Mishnah at the end of the 2nd century. It serves as the foundation for the Talmud.

# TEXT 5

*ETHICS OF THE FATHERS* 4:18

רַבִּי שִׁמְעוֹן בֶּן אֶלְעָזָר אוֹמֵר:

אַל תְּרַצֶּה אֶת חֲבֵרְךָ בְּשַׁעַת כַּעֲסוֹ,
וְאַל תְּנַחֲמֵהוּ בְּשָׁעָה שֶׁמֵּתוֹ מֻטָּל לְפָנָיו,
וְאַל תִּשְׁאַל לוֹ בְּשַׁעַת נִדְרוֹ,
וְאַל תִּשְׁתַּדֵּל לִרְאוֹתוֹ בְּשַׁעַת קַלְקָלָתוֹ.

Rabbi Shimon ben Elazar would say:

Do not attempt to assuage your fellow's anger during the time of his wrath.

Do not attempt to console him at the time when his deceased lies before him.

Do not question him at the time of his vow.

Do not seek to see him at the time of his humiliation.

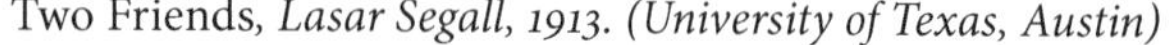

Two Friends, *Lasar Segall, 1913. (University of Texas, Austin)*

# TEXT 6a

ANDREW NEWBERG, M.D., AND MARK ROBERT WALDMAN, *WORDS CAN CHANGE YOUR BRAIN: 12 CONVERSATION STRATEGIES TO BUILD TRUST, RESOLVE CONFLICT, AND INCREASE INTIMACY* (NEW YORK: PLUME, 2013), P. 24

No.

NO.

NO.

NO.

NO!

NO!!!

How did you react when you saw those words? Did your eyebrows rise? Did your muscles tighten? Did you smile or tense your face?

If you were in an fMRI scanner—a huge doughnut-shaped magnet that can take a video of the neural changes happening in your brain—we would record, in less than a second, a substantial increase of activity in your amygdala and the release of dozens of stress-producing hormones and neurotransmitters. These chemicals immediately interrupt the normal functioning of your brain, especially those that are involved with logic, reason, language processing, and communication. . . .

That's how powerful a single negative word or phrase can be. And if you vocalize your negativity, even more stress chemicals will be released, not only in your brain, but in the listener's brain as well.

**ANDREW NEWBERG, MD**
**1966–**

American neuroscientist. Newberg pioneered the study of "neurotheology," the neurological study of religion and spirituality. He is the director of research at the Marcus Institute of Integrative Health and a physician at Jefferson University Hospital in Philadelphia, PA.

# TEXT 6b

IBID., P. 28

Certain positive words—like "peace" or "love"—may actually have the power to alter the expression of genes throughout the brain and body, turning them on and off in ways that lower the amount of physical and emotional stress we normally experience throughout the day.

# TEXT 7

RABBI JOSEPH TELUSHKIN, *REBBE: THE LIFE AND TEACHINGS OF MENACHEM M. SCHNEERSON, THE MOST INFLUENTIAL RABBI IN MODERN HISTORY* (NEW YORK: HARPERCOLLINS PUBLISHER, 2014), PP. 110–113

The Rebbe, both in his public lectures and in his private interactions, emphasized that extraordinary attention must be paid to the words we use. It is hard to know if his caution with words was an acquired trait or one that he always possessed, but four years of research into his life reveal the extraordinary care he took both to avoid using negative words and to avoid speaking negatively of others. . . .

I first became aware of the Rebbe's tendency to avoid using negative language when learning that he never used the term "*beit cholim*," Hebrew for "hospital." I was

**RABBI JOSEPH TELUSHKIN**
**1948–**

Rabbi and author. Telushkin received his ordination at Yeshiva University and a Jewish history degree at Columbia University. He has written many popular books about Judaism, including the best-selling *Jewish Literacy,* and *Rebbe,* a biography of the Lubavitcher Rebbe.

puzzled. What word could he have used, I wondered, as I am unfamiliar with any other term in Hebrew for "hospital."

It turned out that the Rebbe was troubled by "*beit cholim*" because it means, literally, "house of the sick," clearly a discouraging term. The term the Rebbe therefore created was "*beit refuah*," a house of healing. . . .

For the Rebbe, the desire to choose positive words was so deeply ingrained that he hesitated to use words like "evil" even when describing something that was. He did not wish to have negative words or words that had negative associations cross his lips. Instead, to refer to something bad, he would use an expression such as *hefech ha-tov* ("the opposite of good"); to refer to something foolish, he would say *hefech ha-seichel* ("the opposite of intelligent"); to refer to death, he would say *hefech ha-chayyim* ("the opposite of life"); to refer to something unholy, he would say *hefech ha-kedushah* ("the opposite of holiness"). In a usage that sounds almost humorous, he would often speak of a bad person, a *rasha*, as "one who is not a tzaddik" ("one who is not a highly righteous person").

# TEXT 8

TALMUD, MEGILAH 15A

וְאָמַר רַבִּי אֶלְעָזָר אָמַר רַבִּי חֲנִינָא: לְעוֹלָם אַל תְּהִי בִּרְכַּת הֶדְיוֹט קַלָּה בְּעֵינֶיךָ, שֶׁהֲרֵי שְׁנֵי גְדוֹלֵי הַדּוֹר בֵּרְכוּם שְׁנֵי הֶדְיוֹטוֹת וְנִתְקַיְּימָה בָּהֶן, וְאֵלּוּ הֵן: דָּוִד וְדָנִיאֵל. דָּוִד, דְּבָרְכֵיהּ אֲרַוְנָה, דִּכְתִיב, "וַיֹּאמֶר אֲרַוְנָה אֶל הַמֶּלֶךְ, 'ה' אֱלֹקֶיךָ יִרְצֶךָ'" (שְׁמוּאֵל ב כד, כג). דָּנִיאֵל, דְּבָרְכֵיהּ דַּרְיָוֶשׁ, דִּכְתִיב, "אֱלָהָךְ דִּי אַנְתְּ פָּלַח לֵהּ בִּתְדִירָא הוּא יְשֵׁיזְבִינָּךְ" (דָּנִיאֵל ו, יז).

וְאָמַר רַבִּי אֶלְעָזָר אָמַר רַבִּי חֲנִינָא: אַל תְּהִי קִלְלַת הֶדְיוֹט קַלָּה בְּעֵינֶיךָ, שֶׁהֲרֵי אֲבִימֶלֶךְ קִלֵּל אֶת שָׂרָה, "הִנֵּה הוּא לָךְ כְּסוּת עֵינַיִם" (בְּרֵאשִׁית כ, טז), וְנִתְקַיֵּים בְּזַרְעָהּ, "וַיְהִי כִּי זָקֵן יִצְחָק וַתִּכְהֶיןָ עֵינָיו" (בְּרֵאשִׁית כז, א).

Rabbi Elazar said in the name of Rabbi Chanina: Let not the blessing of an ordinary person be unimportant in your eyes, for two great men, David and Daniel, received blessings from ordinary men and they were fulfilled. David was blessed by Araunah, as it is written, "Araunah said to the king, 'May your God favor you'" (II SAMUEL 24:23). Daniel was blessed by Darius, as it is written, "Your God whom you continually serve, He will deliver you" (DANIEL 6:17).

Rabbi Elazar further said in the name of Rabbi Chanina: Let not the curse of an ordinary person be unimportant in your eyes, because Abimelech cursed Sarah, saying, "Behold this is to you a covering of the eyes" (GENESIS 20:16), and this was fulfilled in her progeny, [as it says,] "And it came to pass when Isaac was old and his eyes dimmed" (IBID., 27:1).

# TEXT 9

TALMUD, KETUBOT 8B

לְעוֹלָם אַל יִפְתַּח אָדָם פִּיו לַשָּׂטָן. אָמַר רַב יוֹסֵף, מַאי קְרָא? "כִּסְדוֹם הָיִינוּ לַעֲמוֹרָה דָּמִינוּ" (יְשַׁעְיָהוּ א, ט). מַאי אַהְדַר לֵיהּ? "שִׁמְעוּ דְבַר ה' קְצִינֵי סְדוֹם וְגוֹ'" (שָׁם, י).

One should never speak words that can be employed by Satan. The verses support this, [for when the Jews said: "Had God not spared some of us], we would have been like Sodom; we would have resembled Gomorrah'" (ISAIAH 1:9), the prophet responded: "Hear the word of God, O rulers of Sodom; [listen to the instructions of our God, O people of Gomorrah]" (IBID. 1:10).

The Destruction of Sodom and Gomorrah, *John Martin, 1852. (Laing Art Gallery, Newcastle upon Tyne, England)*

# TEXT 10

MAIMONIDES, *MISHNEH TORAH*, LAWS OF CHARACTER DEVELOPMENT 6:3

מִצְוָה עַל כָּל אָדָם לֶאֱהוֹב אֶת כָּל אֶחָד וְאֶחָד מִיִּשְׂרָאֵל כְּגוּפוֹ, שֶׁנֶּאֱמַר, "וְאָהַבְתָּ לְרֵעֲךָ כָּמוֹךָ" (וַיִּקְרָא יט, יח).

לְפִיכָךְ צָרִיךְ לְסַפֵּר בְּשִׁבְחוֹ וְלָחוּס עַל מָמוֹנוֹ כַּאֲשֶׁר הוּא חָס עַל מָמוֹן עַצְמוֹ וְרוֹצֶה בִּכְבוֹד עַצְמוֹ.

We are obligated to love each and every fellow Jew as we love our own selves, as it is stated, "Love your fellow as yourself" (LEVITICUS 19:18).

Therefore, we must speak the praises of others and be concerned for their property to the same degree that we seek our own honor and are concerned for our own property.

**RABBI MOSHE BEN MAIMON (MAIMONIDES, RAMBAM) 1135–1204**

Halachist, philosopher, author, and physician. Maimonides was born in Córdoba, Spain. After the conquest of Córdoba by the Almohads, he fled Spain and eventually settled in Cairo, Egypt. There, he became the leader of the Jewish community and served as court physician to the vizier of Egypt. He is most noted for authoring the *Mishneh Torah*, an encyclopedic arrangement of Jewish law, and for his philosophical work, *Guide for the Perplexed*. His rulings on Jewish law are integral to the formation of halachic consensus.

## Exercise 3

(a) Think of a loved one and some quality you love about him or her. What words can you say to bring this quality to the fore?

(b) What words can you say about yourself to bring one of your qualities to the fore?

# TEXT 11

TALMUD, TA'ANIT 22A

רַבִּי בְרוֹקָא חוֹזָאָה הֲוָה שְׁכִיחַ בְּשׁוּקָא דְבֵי לֶפֶט, הֲוָה שְׁכִיחַ אֵלִיָּהוּ גַבֵּיהּ. אָמַר לֵיהּ, "אִיכָּא בְּהַאי שׁוּקָא בַּר עָלְמָא דְאָתֵי?" . . .

אַדְּהָכִי וְהָכִי אָתוּ הַנָּךְ תְּרֵי, אָתֵי אָמַר לֵיהּ, "הַנָּךְ נַמִּי בְּנֵי עָלְמָא דְאָתֵי נִינְהוּ".

אֲזַל לְגַבַּיְיהוּ, אָמַר לְהוּ, "מַאי עוֹבָדַיְיכוּ?"

אָמְרוּ לֵיהּ, "אִינָשֵׁי בָּדוּחֵי אֲנַן, מְבַדְּחִינַן עֲצִיבֵי. אִי נַמִּי, כִּי חָזֵינַן בֵּי תְּרֵי דְאִית לְהוּ תִּיגְרָא בַּהֲדַיְיהוּ, טָרְחִינַן וְעָבְדִינַן לְהוּ שְׁלָמָא".

Rabbi Beroka Choza'ah would frequent the market at Bei Lapat where Elijah the Prophet often appeared to him. Rabbi Beroka once asked Elijah, "Is there anyone here who will merit a share in the World to Come?" . . .

While they were talking, two men passed by and Elijah remarked, "These two have a share in the World to Come."

Rabbi Beroka approached them and asked: "What is your occupation?"

They replied: "We are jesters; we make sad people laugh. And when we see two people quarreling, we use humor to make peace between them."

## TEXT 12a

LEVITICUS 19:16

לֹא תֵלֵךְ רָכִיל בְּעַמֶּיךָ, לֹא תַעֲמֹד עַל דַּם רֵעֶךָ, אֲנִי ה'.

Do not go around as a [gossip] peddler amidst your people. Do not idly stand by the shedding of your fellow's blood. I am God.

## TEXT 12b

MAIMONIDES, *MISHNEH TORAH*, LAWS OF CHARACTER DEVELOPMENT 7:2

אֵיזֶהוּ "רָכִיל"? זֶה שֶׁטּוֹעֵן דְּבָרִים וְהוֹלֵךְ מִזֶּה לָזֶה וְאוֹמֵר: "כָּךְ אָמַר פְּלוֹנִי; כָּךְ וְכָךְ שָׁמַעְתִּי עַל פְּלוֹנִי". אַף עַל פִּי שֶׁהוּא אֱמֶת, הֲרֵי זֶה מַחֲרִיב אֶת הָעוֹלָם. יֵשׁ עָוֹן גָּדוֹל מִזֶּה עַד מְאֹד וְהוּא בִּכְלָל לָאו זֶה, וְהוּא לָשׁוֹן הָרָע. וְהוּא: הַמְסַפֵּר בִּגְנוּת חֲבֵירוֹ אַף עַל פִּי שֶׁאוֹמֵר אֱמֶת.

אֲבָל הָאוֹמֵר שֶׁקֶר נִקְרָא: "מוֹצִיא שֵׁם רַע" עַל חֲבֵירוֹ.

Who is a peddler? One who peddles tidbits from one person to another, saying, "So said this one; I heard so and so regarding this one." Even if the information is true, it destroys the world. Included in this prohibition is a sin that is much more severe: *lashon hara*—speaking disparagingly about others, even if speaking the truth.

One who falsely libels his fellow is [guilty of the even greater offense] of slander.

# TEXT 13

TALMUD, ARACHIN 15B

> בְּמַעֲרָבָא אָמְרֵי: לָשׁוֹן תְּלִיתַאי קָטִיל תְּלִיתַאי: הוֹרֵג לַמְסַפְּרוֹ וְלַמְקַבְּלוֹ וּלְאוֹמְרִין עָלָיו.

In the West they say: The third tongue kills three: the one who relays it, the one who receives it, and the one being spoken of.

The Gossips, *Norman Rockwell, 1948. (Norman Rockwell Museum, Massachusetts)*

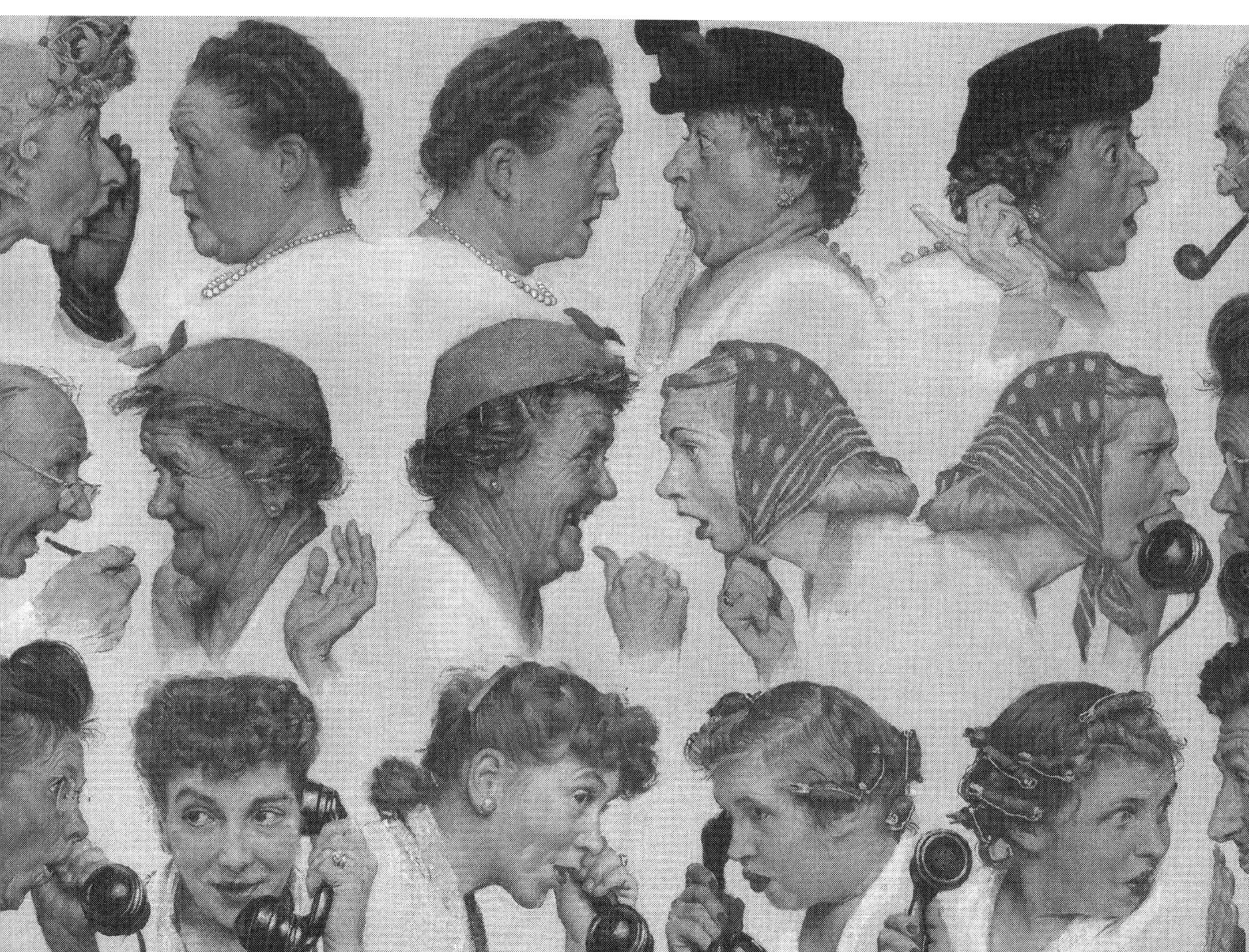

# TEXT 14

THE REBBE, RABBI MENACHEM MENDEL SCHNEERSON, *IGROT KODESH* 7:194–195

זֶה עַתָּה נִתְקַבֵּל מִכְתָּבוֹ . . . וְנִבְהַלְתִּי לְמַה שֶׁכּוֹתֵב בּוֹ עַל עַצְמוֹ, וּכְבָר סִיפַּרְתִּי כַּמָּה פְּעָמִים מַה שֶּׁשָּׁמַעְתִּי מִכְּבוֹד קְדוּשַּׁת מוֹרִי וְחָמִי אַדְמוּ"ר זצוקללה"ה נבג"מ זְכוּתוֹ יָגֵן עָלֵינוּ, שֶׁסִּיפֵּר לִי, אֲשֶׁר נִכְנַס אֵלָיו אֶחָד לְיְחִידוּת וְשָׁאַל תִּיקּוּן עַל אֵיזֶה עִנְיָנִים, וּבִשְׁעַת מַעֲשֶׂה תֵּיאֵר מַצָּבוֹ הָרוּחָנִי בְּאוֹתִיּוֹת מַבְהִילוֹת, וְעָנָהוּ כְּבוֹד קְדוּשַּׁת מוֹרִי וְחָמִי אַדְמוּ"ר אֲשֶׁר יָדוּעַ חוֹמֶר הָעִנְיָן דְּלָשׁוֹן הָרָע שֶׁאָסוּר לְסַפֵּר עַל חֲבֵירוֹ וְגַם עַל עַצְמוֹ, וְדַי לְמֵבִין.

וּלְפִי עֲנִיּוּת דַּעְתִּי יֵשׁ לְהוֹסִיף בֵּיאוּר בָּזֶה עַל פִּי הַיָּדוּעַ בְּכַמָּה מְקוֹמוֹת בְּחִילּוּק דְּלָשׁוֹן הָרָע וּמוֹצִיא שֵׁם רַע.

אֲשֶׁר מוֹצִיא שֵׁם רַע הוּא בְּדִבּוּר שֶׁקֶר, וְלָשׁוֹן הָרָע הוּא אֲפִילּוּ כְּשֶׁמְּסַפֵּר אֱמֶת . . . וּבְכָל זֹאת גָּדוֹל הָאִיסּוּר עַל פִּי הַמְבוֹאָר בַּחֲסִידוּת אֲשֶׁר כְּשֶׁמְּתָאֵר חִסָּרוֹן שֶׁל חֲבֵירוֹ אוֹ אֲפִילּוּ שֶׁל עַצְמוֹ, הֲרֵי לִפְעָמִים תְּכוּפוֹת מַמְשִׁיכִים וּמְגַלִּים אֶת הַחִסָּרוֹן מֵעוֹלָם הַמַּחֲשָׁבָה לְעוֹלָם הַדִּבּוּר, אֲשֶׁר מוּבָן שֶׁכָּל זְמַן שֶׁנִּשְׁאַר בְּמַחֲשָׁבָה אֵינוֹ פּוֹעֵל פְּעוּלָּה, מַה שֶּׁאֵין כֵּן כְּשֶׁבָּא בְּדִבּוּר וּבְמִילָּא מַזִּיק.

I received your letter . . . and I was taken aback by how you described yourself.

I have repeated on several occasions a story that I heard from my father-in-law [Rabbi Yosef Yitschak Schneersohn], the Rebbe, of righteous memory: A person once visited him and requested that the Rebbe prescribe a course of penance for some indiscretions. In the course of the conversation, this person described his personal spiritual state in strongly uncomplimentary terms. The Rebbe responded that it is well known that speaking

**RABBI MENACHEM MENDEL SCHNEERSON**
**1902–1994**

The towering Jewish leader of the 20th century, known as "the Lubavitcher Rebbe," or simply as "the Rebbe." Born in southern Ukraine, the Rebbe escaped Nazi-occupied Europe, arriving in the U.S. in June 1941. The Rebbe inspired and guided the revival of traditional Judaism after the European devastation, impacting virtually every Jewish community the world over. The Rebbe often emphasized that the performance of just one additional good deed could usher in the era of Mashiach. The Rebbe's scholarly talks and writings have been printed in more than 200 volumes.

negatively of another is a grave sin. The same applies to speaking negatively regarding oneself.

In my humble opinion, the notion that one may not speak disparagingly of oneself can be understood by examining the difference between libelous slander and *lashon hara,* both of which are prohibited. Although *lashon hara* describes factual events or flaws, it is nevertheless forbidden. Why would saying the truth be forbidden? The Chasidic texts explain that articulating a person's flaw—another's or one's own—can draw that flaw from the concealed realm of thought to the revealed realm of speech. Once the flaw is in the open, it can cause [greater] harm.

## TEXT 15

MICAH 6:8

> הִגִּיד לְךָ אָדָם מַה טּוֹב וּמָה ה' דּוֹרֵשׁ מִמְּךָ: כִּי אִם עֲשׂוֹת מִשְׁפָּט וְאַהֲבַת
> חֶסֶד וְהַצְנֵעַ לֶכֶת עִם אֱלֹקֶיךָ.

O man, God has told you what is good and what He demands of you: to do justice, to love kindness, and to walk discreetly with your God.

# Exercise 4

Why is privacy important?

Privacy is important because

Compare notes with your neighbor.

# TEXT 16

KATE MURPHY, "WE WANT PRIVACY, BUT CAN'T STOP SHARING," *THE NEW YORK TIMES*, OCT. 4, 2014

A three-year German study ending in 2012 showed that the more people disclosed about themselves on social media, the more privacy they said they desired. The lead author of the study, Sabine Trepte, a professor of media psychology at the University of Hohenheim in Stuttgart, said the paradox indicated participants' dissatisfaction with what they got in return for giving away so much about themselves.

"It's a bad deal because what they get is mainly informational support like maybe a tip for a restaurant or link to an article," she said. "What they don't get is the kind of emotional and instrumental support that leads to well-being, like a shoulder to cry on or someone who will sit by your bedside at the hospital."

# TEXT 17

RABBI JOSEPH B. SOLOVEITCHIK, *DIVREI HAGUT VEHADRACHAH,* P. 174

רֵאשִׁית מִנְעוּרַי לִימְדוּנִי לְהַבְלִיג עַל רִגְשׁוֹתַי וְלֹא לְהַפְגִין אֶת הַמִּתְרַחֵשׁ בְּעוֹלָמִי הָאֶמוֹצְיוֹנָאלִי. אַבָּא מָרִי זַ"ל הָיָה אוֹמֵר, כָּל שֶׁהָרֶגֶשׁ קָדוֹשׁ יוֹתֵר וְכָל שֶׁהוּא אִינְטִימִי יוֹתֵר, טָעוּן הוּא יוֹתֵר גְנִיזָה בְּמַעֲמַקִּים. בָּתֵּי אַבְרָאִי שֶׁבָּהֶם הָאָדָם מַפְעִיל וּמַבְלִיט אֶת הַנַּעֲשֶׂה בִּפְנִימִיּוּתוֹ צְרִיכִים לִהְיוֹת מוּבְדָלִים מִן קוֹדֶשׁ הַקּוֹדָשִׁים שֶׁל הָאָדָם: "וְהִבְדִּילָה הַפָּרוֹכֶת לָכֶם בֵּין הַקּוֹדֶשׁ וּבֵין קוֹדֶשׁ הַקֳּדָשִׁים" (שְׁמוֹת כו, לג). יֶשְׁנָהּ פָּרוֹכֶת סוֹדִית הַמַּבְדִּילָה בֵּין הַפְּנִימִיּוּת וְהַחִיצוֹנִיּוּת, וְאֵיזֶהוּ הַמָּקוֹם הַמְקוּדָּשׁ בְּיוֹתֵר, אִם לֹא קוֹדֶשׁ הַקּוֹדָשִׁים שֶׁל חַיֵּי הָרֶגֶשׁ?

While still a youth, I was taught to contain my feelings and not to publicly display what was transpiring in my emotional world. My father, of blessed memory, would say that the holier and more intimate the feeling, the more it should be hidden from public view. There needs to be a curtain that separates between one's exterior, with which one interacts with the world, and one's Holy of Holies: "And the curtain shall separate for you between the Holy and the Holy of Holies" (EXODUS 26:33). What location is more sacred than the inner sanctum of one's emotional life?

**RABBI JOSEPH B. SOLOVEITCHIK**
**1903–1993**

Talmudist and philosopher. A scion of a famous Lithuanian rabbinical family, Rabbi Soloveitchik was one of the most influential Jewish personalities, leaders, and thinkers of the 20th century. In 1941, he became professor of Talmud at RIETS—Yeshiva University; in this capacity, he ordained more rabbis than anyone else in Jewish history. Among his published works are *Halakhic Man* and *Lonely Man of Faith.*

## TEXT 18

TALMUD, TA'ANIT 8B

שֶׁאֵין הַבְּרָכָה מְצוּיָה . . . אֶלָּא בְּדָבָר הַסָּמוּי מִן הָעַיִן.

Blessing is only found . . . in something hidden from sight.

## TEXT 19

RABBI DAVID ALTSCHULER, *METSUDAT DAVID*, MICAH 6:8

הִגִּיד לְךָ ה' מַה טּוֹב בְּעֵינָיו, וּמַהוּ הַדָּבָר אֲשֶׁר הוּא דוֹרֵשׁ וְשׁוֹאֵל מִמְּךָ. כִּי אִם: רְצוֹנוֹ לוֹמַר, אֵין שׁוּם דָּבָר כִּי אִם - לַעֲשׂוֹת מִשְׁפָּט, וְלֶאֱהוֹב אֶת הַצֶּדֶק, וְלָלֶכֶת עִם אֱלֹקֶיךָ בְּדַרְכֵי מִצְוֹתָיו בִּצְנְעָה, לֹא בְּפִרְסוּם רַב וּלְהִתְיַיהֵר.

God has related to you that which is pleasing in His eyes and that which He demands and asks of you: To do justice, to love righteousness, and to go with your God by observing His commandments discretely, without excessive fanfare or conceit.

**RABBI DAVID ALTSCHULER**
**1687–1769**

Biblical commentator. Rabbi Altschuler, a renowned Polish rabbi, wrote two biblical commentaries that are considered crucial to Bible study: the *Metsudat David* expounds upon the meaning of the text, and *Metsudat Tsion* provides definitions. After he died a martyr's death, his works were published by his son, Rabbi Hillel Altschuler, under the name *Metsudot*.

## KEY POINTS

**1** Anything that is potent has the potential, if misused, to do harm. Because our words are valuable and potent, we are enjoined to be sparing and selective with them.

**2** First and foremost, our choice of words defines and identifies us as wise, or the opposite.

**3** It is important to know *when* to speak, even when the words themselves are perfectly legitimate. When the timing isn't right, well intended words have the potential to be counterproductive.

**4** Our words are important even if we are not talking about another person, and even if there is no listener, inasmuch as our choice of words impacts our perceptions.

**5** Every one of our actions has a corresponding spiritual effect. Words reveal that which previously existed in latent form. Therefore, (a) we should try to confer blessings and good wishes, (b) we should avoid making negative statements, and (c) we should speak the praises of our fellows.

**6** Speaking negatively of others causes spiritual harm to all involved—including the victim of the negative gossip. When we talk negatively about another, we augment and intensify that person's negative qualities.

**7** Humor and small conversations are integral to relationships and bring people closer to each other; they are another demonstration of the power of the spoken word.

**8** Words connect people in an intimate way. This awesome power must be used discriminately, for if we are intimate with everyone, then we are intimate with no one. Disclosing personal information to people outside of one's close circle of family and friends is a misplaced plea for intimacy.

# Additional Readings

## THE COMMUNICATION TRAP

BY MIRIAM ADAHAN, PHD

Many psychologists and advisors are prone to overly optimistic promises about the power of communication to solve all problems. They urge people to, "Share your feelings," and "Talk it out until the problem is resolved." However, this advice can be disastrous! Not everyone values emotional honesty. Not everyone has time to listen. And a lot of people will use your personal information against you!

The reality is that not everyone is capable of "hearing" and empathizing. In fact, empathy is a rare quality, which depends on one's personality type (See my book, *Awareness,* for more on defining personality types).

According to the Myers-Briggs personality system (see *Please Understand Me,* by Keirsey) people are either dominant Thinkers or dominant Feelers. Thinking types (60% of men and 40% of women) have little interest in the world of feelings. They feel no urge to share personal feelings and are irritated and bored by those who do. They often do not even know what they feel and may not care. They are focused on functioning, not feeling. In fact, they feel more powerful and in control when they do not expose their feelings. In contrast, Feeling types (60% women, 40% men) are concerned with their feelings and distressed if they cannot share them. When these two types get together, there is likely to be a lot of mutual frustration, because each has demands which the other cannot meet.

In addition, those suffering from various disorders, such as autism, find it very difficult to understand or value others' feelings. They may think a sad person is angry or that an angry person is happy. Then there are those who are so wrapped up in their own intense feelings that there is no room for anyone else's emotions. Others may be suffering from OCD (obsessive-compulsive disorder), anxiety, depression or rage disorder types. Sharing feelings with any of these types is also likely to end in frustration.

Without feelings, there would be no love, no music, art, poetry or meaningful prayer. But to allow our feelings to rule is like giving the car keys to a three-year-old. Learn not to "emote" when emotional modesty is needed. It is best to inhibit the expression of feelings in the following situations:

- When sharing will overwhelm others. It is "immodest" to share strong feelings of grief, fear or rage, especially around children, who need to see adults as a source of security and strength. To expose these feelings is just as immodest as exposing parts of the body which should be kept covered if the other person is incapable of receiving your pain with empathy and compassion.
- When sharing will exacerbate self-pity and despair. Griping about problems may help people feel better, for about fifteen minutes. After that, "co-rumination," in which both sides complain, will actually lower the mood, especially if the problem has no solution. Unless there is a real crisis, which demands a truly empathetic friend, it is best to limit yourself to fifteen minutes so that you do not sink in bitterness. Then segue into comforting words of faith and trust in G-d.
- When you overdo the sharing and go on for too long. This often happens with people who suffer from Borderline Personality Disorder. Once they have your ear, they can go and on, raging at you for hours for real or imagined sins against them.

**MIRIAM ADAHAN**

Psychologist and therapist. Adahan is the founder of EMETT ("Emotional Maturity Established Through Torah")—a network of self-help groups dedicated to personal growth. She lives in Jerusalem.

- When sharing will lead others to think you are immature, stupid, unstable or histrionic. This is how most Thinking types view Feelings types. Thus, they will say, "You're too sensitive. You're just feeling sorry for yourself. Get over it. Toughen up!" In their presence, act self-confident and full of faith, even if it is just an act.
- When sharing involves humiliation and shaming of others. According to the laws of rebuke, you can share your opinions only if it is done: calmly, lovingly, in a quiet voice, in private and concerning a trait which the other person is capable of changing. It is no use telling someone that they are disorganized, unfriendly, passive, too sensitive, loud, etc. if the person is not capable of—or has no interest in—changing these traits!
- When sharing will cause others to use the information against you. Many people are fired from jobs because they shared their personal woes, either physical or psychological. If you talk to certain people about how irritated you are by their behavior, they will do whatever is distressing to you even more.

So, when you are dealing with a well-intentioned advisor, who keeps urging you to share, take that advice with a grain of salt! Some personality types have great faith in the power of communication. Be wary of these peace-maker types. They will not take your feelings seriously. They believe that all problems can be solved with enough good will and with negotiations. They will urge you to, "Forgive and forget," as if past pain can be quickly wiped out with a bouquet of flowers or a meal in a fancy restaurant. Because they lack psychological depth, their grasp of the problem is superficial. On the positive side, this allows them to be great mediators, as they stay calm and optimistic no matter how upset others are. They will willingly engage in marathon "peace talks," urging opposing sides to make resolutions, contracts and promises. If the sides have integrity and good-will, then this will bring true peace. However, if there is an emotional disturbance or lack of integrity, all promises will soon be broken as soon as there is the slightest irritation. On the negative side, these "peace maker" personality types simply do not believe that evil exists; instead, they assume that meanness or cruelty are temporary anomalies which should be ignored and forgotten as quickly as possible. In fact, they often take the side of the aggressor and blame the victim for not "forgiving and making peace" quickly enough.

**Let's Get Real**

It can be very painful to be in the presence of someone with whom you cannot communicate, especially if the person is demanding, hostile or indifferent—and even more so if you are living with such a person. You can bang your head against the wall and pull your hair out in frustration. You can scream, threaten and engage in acts of vengeance and violence, but this will not change their brain patterns or level of sensitivity. As with all difficulties, use this for your spiritual growth. I suggest doing the following "spiritual games."

1. *Play fish:* Practice being a quiet fish, not talking, merely swimming in the waters of faith and trust in G-d, and repeat words of prayers. Be proud of your self-discipline.
2. *Be proud of your emotional modesty:* Be proud of your ability to realize that it is not always appropriate to expose your feelings.
3. *Count fingers:* With non-communicative people, keep your answers down to five words or less—the fingers of one hand, as in, "That's not comfortable for me." "I cannot multi-task right now."
4. *Turn It Around:* Give yourself whatever it is that you want from the other person that you will never get, such as unconditional love, understanding, appreciation, praise and time.

Chabad.org
Reprinted with permission of the publisher

# WORDS AND STONES

BY RABBI YANKI TAUBER

In Mezhibuzh, the hometown of Rabbi Israel Baal Shem Tov (founder of Chassidism, 1698–1760), two local residents were involved in a bitter dispute. One day, they were angrily shouting at each other in the local synagogue, when one of them cried out: "I'll rip you to pieces with my bare hands!"

The Baal Shem Tov, who was in the synagogue at the time, told his disciples to form a circle, each taking the hand of his neighbor, and to close their eyes. Rabbi Israel himself closed the circle by placing his hands upon the shoulders of the two disciples who stood to his right and his left. Suddenly, the disciples cried out in fright: behind their closed eyelids they saw the angry man actually tearing his fellow apart, just as he had threatened!

Words are like arrows, says the Psalmist, and like smoldering coals. Like arrows, explains the Midrash, for a man stands in one place and his words wreak havoc on another's life many miles away. And like a coal whose outer surface has been extinguished but whose interior remains aflame, so too do malevolent words continue to work their damage long after their external effect has evaporated.

Words kill in many ways. Sometimes they set in motion a chain of events that turn them into a self-fulfilling prophecy; sometimes they are deflected off the object of their venom, to strike some innocent bystander; and sometimes they return like a boomerang to pursue their originator. By whatever route they travel, hateful words inevitably lead to hateful actions, possibly years or even generations after they are uttered. Human nature is such that thoughts strive to find expression in spoken words, and spoken words seek realization in deeds—often by circuitous paths that the original utterer of those words neither desired nor anticipated.

But the power of the word runs deeper than its potential to translate into action. Even if this potential is never realized, even if the spoken words never materialize in the "world of action," they still exist in the higher, more spiritual "world of speech." For man is not only a body, but also a soul; he is not only a physical being, but also a spiritual creature. On the physical plane, spoken words may be significant only as potential actions; in the soul's reality, they *are* actual.

This is what the Baal Shem Tov wished to show his disciples by granting them a glimpse into the world of words inhabited by the souls of the two verbal combatants. He wanted them to understand that every word we utter is *real*, whether or not it comes to fruition in the "world of action" in which our physical self resides. On a higher, more spiritual plane of reality—a reality as real to our soul as the physical reality is to our physical self—our every word is as good (and as bad) as done.

The same is true, of course, in the positive sense: a word of praise, a word of encouragement is as good (and as *good*) as done in the spiritual reality of the soul. Even before a good word has yielded a good deed, it has already had a profound and lasting effect upon the inner state of ourselves and our world.

Chabad.org
Reprinted with permission of the publisher

**RABBI YANKI TAUBER, 1965–**

Chasidic scholar and author. A native of Brooklyn, NY, Rabbi Tauber is an internationally renowned author who specializes in adapting the teachings of the Lubavitcher Rebbe. He is a member of the JLI curriculum development team, and has written numerous articles and books, including *Once Upon a Chassid* and *Beyond the Letter of the Law*.

# *Lesson* 3

## BEHIND THE WORDS

### THE ART OF EFFECTIVE COMMUNICATION

Seventeen Ornamental Letters, *c. 17th century.*
*(Los Angeles County Museum of Art)*

"A man's character may be learned from the adjectives which he habitually uses in conversation."

—Mark Twain

*The simplest messages are often misconstrued in the most unpredictable ways. This is often caused by metamessages that confuse the listeners or shut them down. This lesson explores how distractive elements—such as aggressive rhetoric and the tone of voice—impact on our ability to communicate in a manner that ensures that the listener's takeaway is the same as our intended message.*

# Exercise 1

How many communication gaffes can you detect in the exchange depicted in the video?

| | |
|---|---|
| 1 | |
| 2 | |
| 3 | |
| 4 | |
| 5 | |

# TEXT 1

TALMUD, NEDARIM 66B

הַהוּא בַּר בָּבֶל דְסָלִיק לְאַרְעָא דְיִשְׂרָאֵל, נָסִיב אִיתְּתָא. אָמַר לָהּ: "בַּשִּׁילִי לִי תְּרֵי טַלְפֵי". בַּשִּׁילָא לֵיהּ תְּרֵי טַלְפֵי, רָתַח עֲלָהּ.

לְמָחָר אָמַר לָהּ: "בַּשִּׁילִי לִי גְרִיוָא". בַּשִּׁילָא לֵיהּ גְרִיוָא.

אָמַר לָהּ: "זִילִי אַיְיתִי לִי תְּרֵי בּוּצִינֵי". אָזְלַת וְאַיְיתֵי לֵיהּ תְּרֵי שְׁרַגֵי. אָמַר לָהּ: "זִילִי תַּבְרִי יַתְהוֹן עַל רֵישָׁא דְבָבָא".

הֲוָה יָתִיב בָּבָא בֶּן בּוּטָא אַבָּבָא וְקָא דָאִין דִינָא, אָזְלַת וְתַבְרַת יַתְהוֹן עַל רֵישֵׁיהּ.

A Babylonian immigrated to the Land of Israel and married a local woman. He said to her: "Cook a couple of lentils for me." She [took him literally and] cooked two lentils for him, and he became angry.

On the following day, he said to her: "Cook a *geriva* [a very large measure, far more than what one person could eat] for me." She cooked an actual *geriva*.

He then said to her: "Go and bring me two *butsinei* [melons, in the Babylonian dialect of Aramaic]." She went and brought him two lamps [called *butsinei* in the Israeli dialect of Aramaic]. In anger, he said to her: "Go and break them on the top of the *bava* [a gate, in the Babylonian dialect of Aramaic]."

At that time, the great sage Bava ben Buta was sitting and trying a case. So, the woman went and broke the lamps on his head.

**BABYLONIAN TALMUD**

A literary work of monumental proportions that draws upon the legal, spiritual, intellectual, ethical, and historical traditions of Judaism. The 37 tractates of the Babylonian Talmud contain the teachings of the Jewish sages from the period after the destruction of the 2nd Temple through the 5th century CE. It has served as the primary vehicle for the transmission of the Oral Law and the education of Jews over the centuries; it is the entry point for all subsequent legal, ethical, and theological Jewish scholarship.

# Reflection

Try to recall a conversation that left you feeling frustrated because, despite your best efforts, the person with whom you were speaking didn't really listen and failed to understand the message you were trying to convey.

## Exercise 2

**1** Think of a person whom you find difficult to listen to, whose opinion you tend to summarily reject, and with whom you would never feel comfortable opening up.

What is it about this person's style of communication that triggers the closure of your heart and mind?

**2** Think of a person to whose words you listen closely, whose opinion you tend to respect, and with whom you feel comfortable opening up.

What is it about this person's style of communication that opens and warms your heart and mind?

# TEXT 2

MAIMONIDES, *MISHNEH TORAH*, LAWS OF *TEFILIN*, *MEZUZAH*, AND TORAH SCROLLS 1:19

וְצָרִיךְ לְהִזָּהֵר בִּכְתִיבָתָן, כְּדֵי שֶׁלֹּא תִּדְבַּק אוֹת לְאוֹת, שֶׁכָּל אוֹת שֶׁאֵין הָעוֹר מַקִּיף לָהּ מֵאַרְבַּע רוּחוֹתֶיהָ, פְּסוּלָה.

One must be careful when writing a Torah scroll, *tefilin*, or *mezuzah* to ensure that no letter becomes attached to another. If any letter is not wholly surrounded by blank parchment on all four sides, the scroll is rendered invalid.

**RABBI MOSHE BEN MAIMON (MAIMONIDES, RAMBAM) 1135–1204**

Halachist, philosopher, author, and physician. Maimonides was born in Córdoba, Spain. After the conquest of Córdoba by the Almohads, he fled Spain and eventually settled in Cairo, Egypt. There, he became the leader of the Jewish community and served as court physician to the vizier of Egypt. He is most noted for authoring the *Mishneh Torah*, an encyclopedic arrangement of Jewish law, and for his philosophical work, *Guide for the Perplexed*. His rulings on Jewish law are integral to the formation of halachic consensus.

# TEXT 3a

ECCLESIASTES 9:17

דִּבְרֵי חֲכָמִים בְּנַחַת נִשְׁמָעִים, מִזַּעֲקַת מוֹשֵׁל בַּכְּסִילִים.

The words of the wise, spoken softly, are heard louder than the shout of a foolish ruler.

# TEXT 3b

MAIMONIDES, *MISHNEH TORAH*, LAWS OF CHARACTER DEVELOPMENT 5:7

תַּלְמִיד חָכָם לֹא יְהֵא צוֹעֵק וְצוֹוֵחַ בְּשַׁעַת דִּבּוּרוֹ כַּבְּהֵמוֹת וְכַחַיּוֹת, וְלֹא יַגְבִּיהַּ קוֹלוֹ בְּיוֹתֵר, אֶלָּא דִּבּוּרוֹ בְּנַחַת עִם כָּל הַבְּרִיּוֹת.

A scholar should not shout or shriek while speaking, like the cattle and wild beasts, or speak with a raised voice. Rather, a scholar should speak gently to all people.

## QUESTION FOR DISCUSSION

When a person speaks in a forceful tone, what metamessage is the speaker communicating?

## QUESTION FOR DISCUSSION

How is the listener likely to react?

# TEXT 4

RABBI MENACHEM ME'IRI, AVOT 2:5

"וְלֹא הַקַּפְּדָן מְלַמֵּד" (אָבוֹת ב, ה). רְצוֹנוֹ לוֹמַר, מִי שֶׁמַּקְפִּיד וְכַעֲסָן וּמְדַקְדֵּק בְּהַנְהָגַת תַּלְמִידָיו יוֹתֵר מִדַּאי. שֶׁהַקְפָּדָתוֹ יְמַנָּעֵהוּ מִהְיוֹת דְבָרָיו עֲרֵבִים לְשׁוֹמְעָיו, שֶׁלֹּא יוּכְלוּ לָשֵׂאת וְלָתֵת עִמּוֹ בְּמִשְׁנָתָם כָּרָאוּי.

"An irritable person ought not be a teacher" (ETHICS OF THE FATHERS 2:5). One who is irritable, short-tempered, and overly exacting regarding the students' behavior [should not teach]. Such a harsh disposition prevents the students from seeing the beauty in the teachings, for they will be too intimidated to enter into a dialogue about the subject matter.

**RABBI MENACHEM ME'IRI**
**1249–1310**

Talmudist and author. Me'iri was born in Provence, France. His monumental work, *Beit Habechirah,* summarizes in a lucid style the discussions of the Talmud along with the commentaries of the major subsequent rabbis. Despite its stature, the work was largely unknown for many generations, and thus has had less influence on subsequent halachic development.

# TEXT 5

TALMUD, BERACHOT 63B

"וְדִבֶּר ה' אֶל מֹשֶׁה פָּנִים אֶל פָּנִים" (שְׁמוֹת לג, יא). אָמַר רַבִּי יִצְחָק: אָמַר לוֹ הַקָּדוֹשׁ בָּרוּךְ הוּא לְמֹשֶׁה, "מֹשֶׁה! אֲנִי וְאַתָּה נַסְבִּיר פָּנִים בַּהֲלָכָה".

"God spoke to Moses, face-to-face" (EXODUS 33:11). Rabbi Yitschak explained: God said to Moses, "Moses! Let us exhibit cheerful faces to one another as we study the law."

Exodus #17, And Moses Went Up Unto Mount Sinai. And the Lord Descended in the Cloud,
*Peter Lipman-Wulf, ink on paper, 1960. (Leo Baeck Institute at the Center for Jewish History, New York)*

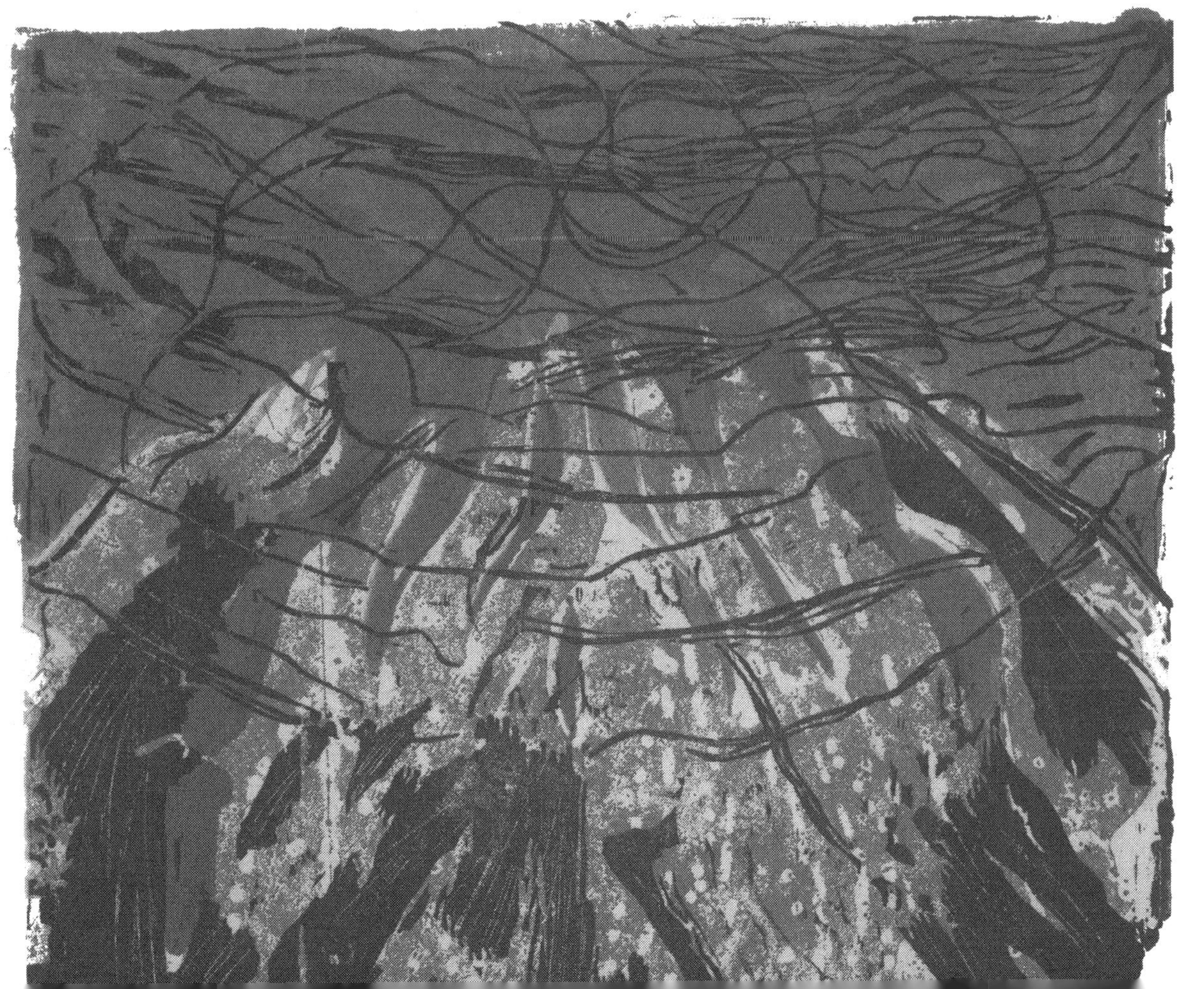

# TEXT 6

RABBI YOSEF YITSCHAK SCHNEERSOHN, *PRINCIPLES OF EDUCATION AND GUIDANCE*, CH. 5

הַמְחַנֵּךְ וְהַמַּדְרִיךְ צָרִיךְ לָדַעַת כִּי לֹא רַק פִּתְגָמִים מַתְאִימִים לְעִנְיָנֵי הוֹרָאוֹתָיו נוֹגְעִים בְּעִיקְּרֵי תּוֹעֶלֶת הַחִינּוּךְ וְהַהַדְרָכָה, אֶלָּא גַּם אוֹפֶן בִּיטּוּי הַפִּתְגָמִים, אִם בְּנִימוּס וּמְתִינוּת אוֹ בְּהִתְרַגְּשׁוּת וְזִלְזוּל, נוֹגֵעַ בִּיסוֹדֵי תּוֹעֶלֶת הַחִינּוּךְ וְהַהַדְרָכָה . . .

רַבִּים מֵהַמְחַנְּכִים וְהַמַּדְרִיכִים טוֹעִים בָּזֶה מַה שֶּׁחוֹשְׁבִים אֲשֶׁר בְּהִתְרַגְּשׁוּת בְּקוֹל רַעַם וָרַעַשׁ יַגִּיעוּ לְמַטְּרָתָם בְּחִינּוּךְ וְהַדְרָכָה, וּמֵהֶם מִתְנַפְּלִים עַל הַמְחוּנָּךְ וְהַמּוּדְרָךְ בְּדִבְרֵי רוֹגֶז בִּדְבָרִים קָשִׁים כְּגִידִים וְיֶחָרְפֶנּוּ וִיגַדְּפֶנּוּ.

וּבֶאֱמֶת הִנֵּה גַּם אִם לְשָׁעָה מִתְרַגֵּשׁ הַמְחוּנָּךְ וְהַמּוּדְרָךְ מִלַּפִּידֵי אֵשׁ אִמְרֵי פִּי הַמְחַנֵּךְ וְהַמַּדְרִיךְ וּלְבָבוֹ מִתְכַּוֵּוץ מִצַּעַר וּלְפְעָמִים הִנֵּה גַּם יִבְכֶּה בְּמַר נַפְשׁוֹ, הִנֵּה חִינּוּךְ וְהַדְרָכָה זוּ לֹא יָבִיאוּ שׁוּם תּוֹעֶלֶת וְכַחֲלוֹם יָעוּף.

An educator or counselor must understand that not only is it important to appropriately phrase one's words, but that the manner in which the words are expressed—with politeness and patience or with agitation and derision—profoundly impacts the effectiveness of the educational message. . . .

Many educators and counselors err in this area. They imagine that their emotional outbursts that are accompanied by much commotion and shouting help them achieve their educational goals. Some assault their students with harsh and angry words and berate and insult them.

**RABBI YOSEF YITSCHAK SCHNEERSOHN (RAYATS, FRIERDIKER REBBE, PREVIOUS REBBE) 1880–1950**

Chasidic rebbe, prolific writer, and Jewish activist. Rabbi Yosef Yitschak, the 6th leader of the Chabad movement, actively promoted Jewish religious practice in Soviet Russia and was arrested for these activities. After his release from prison and exile, he settled in Warsaw, Poland, from where he fled Nazi occupation, and arrived in New York in 1940. Settling in Brooklyn, Rabbi Schneersohn worked to revitalize American Jewish life. His son-in law, Rabbi Menachem Mendel Schneerson, succeeded him as the leader of the Chabad movement.

In truth, however, even if the pupil is temporarily upset by the fiery words of the educator or counselor, this type of education yields no lasting benefit whatsoever. This is true even if the pupil's heart contracts from pain, and he or she cries bitter tears. Any [temporary positive] effect will vanish like a fleeting dream.

## TEXT 7

RABBI SHLOMO GANZFRIED, *KITSUR SHULCHAN ARUCH* 29:8

כְּבַר כָּתַבְנוּ מַאֲמַר יְהוּדָה בֶּן תֵּימָא (אָבוֹת ה, כ), "הֱוֵי עַז כַּנָּמֵר כוּ'", שֶׁלֹּא יִתְבַּיֵּשׁ מִפְּנֵי בְּנֵי אָדָם הַמַּלְעִיגִים עָלָיו בַּעֲבוֹדַת הַבּוֹרֵא יִתְבָּרַךְ שְׁמוֹ. אֲבָל מִכָּל מָקוֹם, לֹא יַעֲנֶה אוֹתָם דִּבְרֵי עַזּוּת, שֶׁלֹּא יִקְנֶה קִנְיָן בְּנַפְשׁוֹ לִהְיוֹת עַז פָּנִים, אֲפִילוּ שֶׁלֹּא בִּמְקוֹם עֲבוֹדָתוֹ יִתְבָּרַךְ שְׁמוֹ.

We have already quoted the statement of Yehudah ben Teima (ETHICS OF THE FATHERS 5:20): "Be bold as a leopard," which teaches us not to be embarrassed in the face of people who mock us for serving God. Nevertheless, we should not reply to our detractors with scorn, so that we don't become habituated to responding with brazenness in other areas of life.

**RABBI SHLOMO GANZFRIED**
**1804–1886**

Rabbi and halachic authority. Rabbi Ganzfried was born in Uzhhorod (today part of Ukraine), and after being orphaned at a very young age, he was adopted by Uzhhorod's chief rabbi, Rabbi Tzvi Hirsh Heller. Rabbi Ganzfried is best known for his *Kitsur Shulchan Aruch*, a user-friendly summary of the Shulchan Aruch and the observations of subsequent halachic commentators. This highly acclaimed work quickly became a classic, a mainstay in every Jewish home.

# TEXT 8a

GENESIS 27:18–19

וַיָּבֹא אֶל אָבִיו, וַיֹּאמֶר "אָבִי".

וַיֹּאמֶר, "הִנֶּנִּי, מִי אַתָּה בְּנִי?"

וַיֹּאמֶר יַעֲקֹב אֶל אָבִיו, "אָנֹכִי עֵשָׂו בְּכֹרֶךָ, עָשִׂיתִי כַּאֲשֶׁר דִּבַּרְתָּ אֵלָי. קוּם
נָא שְׁבָה וְאָכְלָה מִצֵּידִי בַּעֲבוּר תְּבָרְכַנִּי נַפְשֶׁךָ".

Jacob came to his father and said, "Father!"

"Here I am," Isaac said. "Who are you, my son?"

Jacob said to his father, "I am Esau, your firstborn. I have done as you have bid me. Please rise and sit down and eat of my game, so that your soul will bless me."

# TEXT 8b

IBID., 27:31

> וַיַּעַשׂ גַּם הוּא מַטְעַמִּים, וַיָּבֵא לְאָבִיו. וַיֹּאמֶר לְאָבִיו, "יָקֻם אָבִי וְיֹאכַל מִצֵּיד בְּנוֹ, בַּעֲבֻר, תְּבָרְכַנִּי נַפְשֶׁךָ".

Esau, too, had made tasty foods, and he brought them to his father. He said to his father, "Rise, Father! Eat of your son's game, so that your soul will bless me."

# TEXT 8c

RASHI, GENESIS 27:22

> קוֹל יַעֲקֹב: שֶׁמְּדַבֵּר בִּלְשׁוֹן תַּחֲנוּנִים, "קוּם נָא". אֲבָל עֵשָׂו בִּלְשׁוֹן קַנְטוּרְיָא דִּבֵּר, "יָקֻם אָבִי!"

"It is Jacob's voice" (GENESIS 27:22), for he speaks reverently: "Please rise." Esau, on the other hand, spoke harshly, "Rise, Father!"

**RABBI SHLOMO YITSCHAKI (RASHI) 1040–1105**

Most noted biblical and Talmudic commentator. Born in Troyes, France, Rashi studied in the famed *yeshivot* of Mainz and Worms. His commentaries on the Pentateuch and the Talmud, which focus on the straightforward meaning of the text, appear in virtually every edition of the Talmud and Bible.

# TEXT 9

KERRY PATTERSON, *CRUCIAL CONVERSATIONS: TOOLS FOR TALKING WHEN STAKES ARE HIGH* (NEW YORK: MCGRAW-HILL, 2002), PP. 143–144

Talking tentatively simply means that we tell our story as a story rather than disguising it as a hard fact. "Perhaps you were unaware . . ." suggests that you're not absolutely certain. "In my opinion . . ." says you're sharing an opinion and no more.

When sharing a story, strike a blend between confidence and humility. Share in a way that expresses appropriate confidence in your conclusions while demonstrating that, if called for, you want your conclusions challenged. To do so, change "The fact is" to "In my opinion." Swap "Everyone knows that" for "I've talked to three of our suppliers who think that." Soften "It's clear to me" to "I'm beginning to wonder if."

Why soften the message? Because we're trying to add meaning to the pool, not force it down people's throats. If we're too forceful, the information won't make it into the pool. One of the ironies of dialogue is that, when talking with those holding opposing opinions, the more convinced and forceful you act, the more resistant others become. Speaking in absolute and overstated terms does not increase your influence, it decreases it. The converse is also true—the more tentatively you speak, the more open people become to your opinions.

**KERRY PATTERSON**

Author of many articles and training programs on communication for success, Patterson cofounded Interact Performance Systems where he served as vice president of research and development for ten years. Patterson coauthored several best-selling titles, including *Change Anything* (2011).

# Figure 3.1

Examples of Statements That We Should Usually Avoid

| |
|---|
| "This is what went wrong." |
| "This is what we have to do." |
| "That won't work." |
| "This is stupid." |
| "This is the best idea!" |

# TEXT 10

RABBI YOSEF CHAIM OF BAGHDAD, *BEN YEHOYADA*, BERACHOT 63B

נִרְאֶה לִי בְּסִייַעְתָּא דִשְׁמַיָּא, שֶׁנָּתַן לוֹ רְשׁוּת שֶׁיֹּאמַר לְפָנָיו חִידּוּשׁ אֲשֶׁר יִתְחַדֵּשׁ בְּשִׂכְלוֹ בְּאֵיזֶה טַעַם וּסְבָרָה שֶׁמּוֹצֵא בְּדִבְרֵי תּוֹרָה שֶׁלּוֹמֵד לְפָנָיו יִתְבָּרַךְ. וְלֹא יֹאמַר, "אֵיךְ לִפְנֵי הַשֵּׁם יִתְבָּרַךְ, שֶׁהוּא אֱלֹקֵי אֱמֶת אֲשֶׁר הַדְּבָרִים מִמֶּנּוּ יָצְאוּ וְנֶחְצְבוּ, אוֹמֵר דָּבָר מַה שֶּׁנִּרְאֶה לְדַעְתִּי?"

וְרָצָה הַשֵּׁם יִתְבָּרַךְ בְּכַךְ, שֶׁיִּהְיֶה מְכַוֵּין עַל הָאֱמֶת מִדַּעְתּוֹ.

**RABBI YOSEF CHAIM OF BAGHDAD (*BEN ISH CHAI*) 1834–1909**

Sefardic halachist and kabbalist. Rabbi Yosef Chaim succeeded his father as chief rabbi of Baghdad in 1859, and is best known as author of his halachic work, *Ben Ish Chai*, by which title he is also known. Also popular is his commentary on the homiletical sections of the Talmud, called *Ben Yehoyada*.

It appears to me that [with these words,] God gave Moses permission to express any thoughts and novel ideas that occurred to him while he learned Torah from the mouth of God. "Do not say," God said to Moses, "'How can I express my opinion before the Almighty, the God of Truth, the Author of the Torah?'"

God wanted Moses to feel free to express his opinions, for He wanted Moses to arrive at the truth of his own accord [as opposed to submitting to God's superior wisdom].

# TEXT 11

RABBI CHAIM CHIZKEYAHU MEDINI, *SEDEI CHEMED* (VOL. 9), *KELALEI HAPOSKIM* 16:1

מָצִינוּ שֶׁכָּתְבוּ הַפּוֹסְקִים בִּלְשׁוֹן אֶפְשָׁר, וְהַבָּאִים אַחֲרָיו כָּתְבוּ שֶׁכֵּן דַעְתּוֹ בְּוַדַאי, וּפָסְקוּ הַלָּכָה כֵּן . . . דְאֵינוֹ לָשׁוֹן סָפֵק, אֶלָּא דֶרֶךְ עֲנָוָה הוּא לִכְתּוֹב כֵּן.

We find that halachic authorities will state an opinion while using the word "*efshar*" (perhaps this is so), and then subsequent halachic authorities will cite the opinion as the unequivocal view of the earlier sage and base their rulings on this opinion. . . . This is because *efshar* doesn't [necessarily] imply doubt; rather, it is an unpretentious way to express oneself.

**RABBI CHAIM CHIZKEYAHU MEDINI**
**1833–1905**

Scholar and prolific author. A Jerusalem native, Rabbi Medini was born into a distinguished Sephardic family. He served as the rabbi of Constantinople and later in the Crimea, during which time he authored many volumes of Torah scholarship. His most famous work is the 18-volume *Sedei Chemed*, a comprehensive encyclopedia of the Talmud. He eventually returned to Israel where he passed away in 1905.

Jüdische Szene *(Jewish Scene), Carl Schleicher, oil on panel, 19th century.*

# Figure 3.2

Words to Be Wary Of

| | |
|---|---|
| Absolutely | Must |
| Always | Never |
| Can't | Perfect |
| Certainly | Worst |

# Figure 3.3

A Rebbe Edits

"His father replied, 'In his prayers, a Jew requests of G-d to fulfill all his needs and he is certain that his request will be granted, for it is directed to G-d Who is the Father of every Jew - young or old, man or woman. When you ask something of a father ~~you must~~ it is proper first to cause him satisfaction. The greatest satisfaction to a father is when his children, who are many and diverse, live amongst each other with brotherly love, loving one another as one's self - VIOHAVTO LIRAIACHO KOMOCHO.

FROM THE SECRETARIAT OF THE LUBAVITCHER REBBE

RABBI MENACHEM M. SCHNEERSON

In response to numerous inquiries about the special ~~instructions~~ suggestions ~~announced by~~ contained in the Rebbe ~~in~~ his public address on the Sabbath preceding the month of Av, concerning the 'Nine Days' (which commemorate the destruction of the Holy Temple in Jerusalem of old), we publish the following excerpt from his talk:

# TEXT 12

RABBI MOSHE BEN NACHMAN, NUMBERS 13:22

בַּעֲבוּר שֶׁצִּוָּה אוֹתָם לִרְאוֹת "הַשְּׁמֵנָה הִיא אִם רָזָה", הֵשִׁיבוּ לוֹ כִּי הִיא שְׁמֵנָה, "וְגַם זָבַת חָלָב וּדְבַשׁ הִיא". וְעַל שְׁאֵלָתוֹ "הֲיֵשׁ בָּהּ עֵץ אִם אַיִן", הֵשִׁיבוּ לוֹ "וְזֶה פִּרְיָהּ", כִּי כֵן צִוָּה אוֹתָם לְהַרְאוֹתוֹ. וְהִנֵּה, בְּכָל זֶה אָמְרוּ אֱמֶת וְהֵשִׁיבוּ עַל מַה שֶּׁנִּצְטַוּוּ.

וְהָיָה לָהֶם לֵאמֹר שֶׁהָעָם הַיּוֹשֵׁב עָלֶיהָ עַז וְהֶעָרִים בְּצוּרוֹת, כִּי יֵשׁ לָהֶם לְהָשִׁיב אִמְרֵי אֱמֶת לְשׁוֹלְחָם, כִּי כֵן צִוָּה אוֹתָם "הֶחָזָק הוּא הֲרָפֶה, הַבְּמַחֲנִים אִם בְּמִבְצָרִים".

אֲבָל רִשְׁעָם בְּמִלַּת "אֶפֶס", שֶׁהִיא מוֹרָה עַל דָּבָר אֶפֶס וְנִמְנָע מִן הָאָדָם, שֶׁאִי אֶפְשָׁר בְּשׁוּם עִנְיָן.

Because Moses instructed the spies to report whether the Land was fertile or lean, they responded that the Land was fertile, "and it flows with milk and honey." In response to Moses's question, "Are there trees in the Land or not?", they responded by displaying the fruit of the Land, as they were instructed. In all this, they spoke truthfully and responded accurately to the questions they were posed.

They were also justified when they asserted that "the people who inhabit the Land are mighty, and the cities are extremely huge and fortified." Moses, who sent them on the mission, had asked them to ascertain whether the Canaanites are "strong or weak," and whether "they

**RABBI MOSHE BEN NACHMAN (NACHMANIDES, RAMBAN) 1194–1270**

Scholar, philosopher, author, and physician. Nachmanides was born in Spain and served as leader of Iberian Jewry. In 1263, he was summoned by King James of Aragon to a public disputation with Pablo Cristiani, a Jewish apostate. Though Nachmanides was the clear victor of the debate, he had to flee Spain because of the resulting persecution. He moved to Israel and helped reestablish communal life in Jerusalem. He authored a classic commentary on the Pentateuch and a commentary on the Talmud.

reside in cities which are unprotected or fortified." They were obliged to respond truthfully.

Their evil, however, was in adding the word "impossible" (*efes*): "*It is impossible* [to conquer the Land because] the people who inhabit the Land are mighty, and the cities are extremely huge and fortified."

Untitled, *Walls of Jericho, Reb Shalom of Safed (1896–1980), color lithograph. (The Trout Gallery, Dickinson College)*

# Figure 3.4

More Words to Be Wary Of

| | |
|---|---|
| Best | Really |
| Exceedingly | So (as in "so beautiful") |
| Extremely | Too (as in "too loud") |
| Least | Very |
| Most | Words that end with "est" (e.g., biggest, filthiest, greatest, smartest, strangest) |

# TEXT 13

MIKI KASHTAN, "THE PARADOX OF WHY," *PSYCHOLOGY TODAY*, APRIL 26, 2013

Even though we want to know why, asking for it directly is not usually a reliable strategy to get a useful answer. The reason for this challenge is that we are so habituated to associate a "why" question with being reproached or shamed. Growing up, for example, being asked: "Why did you do that?" often comes with a stern look and frustrated tone. Whether or not the person who asked intended to frighten us, that is often the effect. Since, in addition, we rarely tell people why we ask "why" questions, the tendency to hear them as blame and accusation is reinforced.

Power differences only exacerbate this phenomenon. The person with more power is more likely to ask the "why" question of the person with less power, and more likely to be heard as blaming. The person with less power is not likely to ask the "why" question in the first place, usually because of fear, sometimes because of disconnection.

**MIKI KASHTAN, PHD**

Sociologist and author. Kashtan is a cofounder of the Bay Area Nonviolent Communication Center and a consultant at the Center for Efficient Collaboration. She received her doctorate in sociology from the University of California—Berkeley. She has authored three books, including *Reweaving Our Human Fabric: Working Together to Create a Nonviolent Future* (2015).

# Figure 3.5

Questions to Be Wary Of

| "What do you think you're doing?" |
|---|
| "Why did you do that?" |
| "How could you have . . .?" |
| "What were you thinking when you . . .?" |

# Exercise 3

**1** *Parent to teenager*: "Your dirty clothes are all over the floor again! Why do you always do that? You don't have the slightest regard for cleanliness!"

How many communication flaws does this statement contain?

1

2

3

4

5

Reword the statement so that it is nonaggressive and productive:

**2** *To spouse*: "Honey, I've been thinking about our argument last night. It was an unmitigated disaster! I figured out what went wrong, and I have an idea for moving forward. I know you'll like it."

How many communication flaws does this statement contain?

1

2

3

4

5

Reword the statement so that it is nonaggressive and productive:

# TEXT 14

RABBI BECHAYE BEN ASHER, *KAD HAKEMACH, RESHUT* (4)

"אַל תְּבַהֵל עַל פִּיךָ . . ." (קֹהֶלֶת ה, א). בָּא הַכָּתוּב הַזֶּה לְהַזְהִיר עַל הָאָדָם שֶׁלֹּא יִהְיֶה נִמְהָר אַחַר דְּבָרָיו לְהוֹצִיאָם מִפִּיו פִּתְאוֹם, אֶלָּא בְּמָתוּן וְאַחַר הִתְבּוֹנְנוּת. וְזֶהוּ שֶׁאָמַר, "אַל תְּבַהֵל עַל פִּיךָ", כִּי הַמְדַבֵּר בְּלֹא קְדִימַת מַחֲשָׁבָה, הַהוּא יִקָּרֵא נִבְהָל.

"Be not rash with your mouth . . ." (ECCLESIASTES 5:1). This verse admonishes us not to speak impulsively. Rather, we should speak deliberately and only after thoughtful consideration. This is the meaning of the words, "Be not rash with your mouth," for the rash person is one who speaks without prior deliberation.

**RABBEINU BECHAYE BEN ASHER**
**CA. 1265–1340**

Biblical commentator. Rabbeinu Bechaye lived in Spain and was a disciple of Rabbi Shlomo ben Aderet, known as Rashba. He is best known for his multifaceted commentary on the Torah, which interprets the text on literal, *midrashic*, philosophical, and kabbalistic levels. Rabbeinu Bechaye also wrote *Kad Hakemach*, a work on philosophy and ethics.

Exodus #15, Thou Shall Smite the Rock, and There Shall Water Come out, That the People May Drink, *Peter Lipman-Wulf, ink on paper, 1960. (Leo Baeck Institute at the Center for Jewish History, New York)*

# TEXT 15

MAIMONIDES, *MISHNEH TORAH,* LAWS OF CHARACTER DEVELOPMENT 2:3

הַכַּעַס, דֵעָה רָעָה הִיא עַד לִמְאוֹד, וְרָאוּי לְאָדָם שֶׁיִתְרַחֵק מִמֶנָּה עַד הַקָצֶה הָאַחֵר, וִילַמֵד עַצְמוֹ שֶׁלֹא יִכְעֹס, וַאֲפִילוּ עַל דָבָר שֶׁרָאוּי לִכְעֹס עָלָיו.

Anger is an exceptionally bad quality. It is proper to distance oneself from anger to the furthest extreme and train oneself not to become angry, even in response to an incident that rightfully calls for anger.

# TEXT 16

*SIFREI*, MATOT 5

בִּשְׁלוֹשָׁה מְקוֹמוֹת בָּא לִכְלָל כַּעַס וּבָא לִכְלָל טָעוּת.

Moses became angry on three occasions, and in each instance, it led him to err.

***SIFREI***

An early rabbinic Midrash on the biblical books of Numbers and Deuteronomy. *Sifrei* focuses mostly on matters of law, as opposed to narratives and moral principles. According to Maimonides, this halachic Midrash was authored by Rav, a 3rd century Babylonian Talmudic sage.

# Figure 3.6

How to Prepare for an Important Conversation

**1** Formulate in your mind the words you will (and will not) use.

**2** Be sure that you're not tense or emotionally charged.

**3** Establish a friendly environment by opening the conversation with pleasant small talk.

## KEY POINTS

**1** Our every communication contains two messages: the literal meaning of the words and the "color" of those words. The color is generally more powerful than the content of the words. When we don't feel heard, it is often because the coloring of our words renders them unable to be heard.

**2** The tone we use when communicating conveys emotion, attitude, interest, priority, emphasis, etc. Speaking with the wrong "color" may lead to confusion or even conflict.

**3** The Torah instructs us to speak in a gentle and soft tone. Speaking with a forceful tone is a form of disrespect and aggression and will generally evoke resistance or unhealthy and unsustainable submission.

**4** The essence of aggressive communication is the attempt to impose one's views on another, even if speaking politely and in a soft tone. Effective communication is colored with tentativeness, humility, and an openness to hear an opposing viewpoint.

**5** A subtle form of communication aggressiveness is the overuse of superlatives. Superlatives tend to take factual information and add an element of opinion—but without identifying it as such.

**6** We should only ask a question if we are genuinely looking for an answer. To make a statement in a questioning manner is dishonest and a form of aggressive speech.

**7** Before engaging in an important conversation, it is important to (a) formulate our message and words in advance, (b) be sure that we are calm and relaxed, and (c) generate an amiable atmosphere.

**8** We should strive to listen to others and accept the truths they impart regardless of the manner in which the message was transmitted.

# Additional Readings

## POWERFUL BIBLICAL STATEMENTS: LESSONS IN COMMUNICATION FOR TODAY'S LEADERSHIP

BY HERSHEY H. FRIEDMAN, PHD, AND LINDA W. FRIEDMAN, PHD

One of the most important prerequisites for effective leadership is powerful communication. This has been observed throughout all of human history, and examples of powerful communication may be found even in one of the oldest documents of record, the Hebrew Bible. What makes a powerful statement? Is it the message or the medium? Is a powerful communicator simply a talented wordsmith, or is the content of the communication paramount?

This paper will examine some of the most powerful statements in the Hebrew Bible. That these statements still resonate today can provide guidance to all of us, especially those in leadership positions. The Biblical statements chosen for study in this paper are both powerful and poignant. Although these passages were admittedly selected according to the subjective opinions of the authors, many are highly cited, by both religious leaders and secular. For example, the verse in Leviticus (25:10), "Proclaim liberty throughout all the land unto all the inhabitants thereof," is inscribed on the Liberty Bell and is a powerful message for humankind. Frederick Douglass (1852) used Psalm 137 to denounce slavery. The verse in question "How can we sing the Lord's song in a strange land?" is mournful and gut-wrenching, whether it stands on its own or in context:

> *By the rivers of Babylon, there we sat down. Yea! We wept when we remembered Zion. We hanged our harps upon the willows in the midst thereof. For there, they that carried us away captive, required of us a song; and they who wasted us required of us mirth, saying, Sing us one of the songs of Zion. How can we sing the Lord's song in a strange land? If I forget thee, O Jerusalem, let my right hand forget her cunning. If I do not remember thee, let my tongue cleave to the roof of my mouth.*

The "Let my people go!" proclamation from Exodus (5:1) became a famous African-American spiritual and a mantra of the civil rights movement. As the battle cry of Soviet Jewish dissidents and refuseniks, it helped destroy Communism. Jews all over the world, and many non-Jews, rallied to that passionate appeal. Muravchik (2010) asserts that the:

> *. . . dramatization of the Soviet refusal to let people leave, a denial of freedom matched by few if any non-Communist dictatorships, served as a powerful reminder of the nature of our foe and, even, of the forgotten virtues of Western democratic civilization.*

As noted above, many of the passages included herein are highly cited. They may have been quoted in the speeches of effective, powerful and/or charismatic leaders. Many project passion and, almost by the very fact of their inclusion in this sort of collection, they are memorable. In examining the passages culled for

**HERSHEY H. FRIEDMAN, PHD**

Professor Friedman is a professor of business and marketing and the director of business programs at Brooklyn College. His areas of expertise include business ethics and corporate social responsibility.

**LINDA W. FRIEDMAN, PHD**

Linda Friedman is a professor in the department of Information Systems and Statistics at Baruch College in New York. Her fields of interest include business statistics, object-oriented programming, and humor studies. She writes fiction, non-fiction, and poetry, and four of her books have been published.

this project, the authors looked for some sort of commonality or paradigm or classification scheme that could be useful in drawing lessons from these powerful, historic statements. It was determined that, for a passage to be memorable and powerful, it could be categorized on one or more of three dimensions: content, language and simplicity. Clearly, these categories are not mutually exclusive and some passages could easily have been selected to represent one dimension as well as another.

**Simplicity**

Some of the most powerful and memorable passages in all of Scriptures are short and pithy, rendered in a very few words. The first three examined here are also among the most effective and successful messages in all of Scriptures.

A proclamation made by one ancient prophet, Jonah, was so potent that an entire empire changed its ways. Jonah's reluctant prophecy was quite brief, using only five Hebrew words (Jonah 3:4): "Forty more days and Nineveh will be overthrown." Jonah made the people believe that if they did not change their ways they were doomed and was, thus, instrumental in getting the people of Nineveh to repent.

For brevity and passion, there is not much that can compete with Moses' prayer to God on behalf of his sister Miriam (Numbers 12:13): "And Moses cried unto the Lord, saying, Heal her now, O God, I beseech Thee." This simple prayer may be even more simply translated, thus: "O God, please. Heal her please." This statement is powerful in its brevity—more so, even, in Hebrew, a five-word cry to God. One would have expected Moses to be upset with Miriam, who, after badmouthing Moses for marrying a Cushite woman was punished by God with *tzaraat* (an awful skin disease usually mistranslated as leprosy). Instead, his prayer on behalf of her is probably the most moving prayer in the entire Hebrew Bible. It is also the briefest prayer. In Hebrew, it consists of only five simple words, using all of 11 letters.

"Shall the Judge of the whole world not act justly?" This bold and sassy statement by Abraham to God (Genesis 18:25) makes it clear that justice is one of the pillars on which the entire world rests. Abraham was upset that God was planning to destroy Sodom and Gomorrah. Even God has to be able to justify his actions. This verse makes it clear that a country that is not concerned with justice may forfeit its right to exist.

"Justice, and only justice, you shall pursue . . ." This passage in Deuteronomy (16:20) continues ". . . so that you will live and possess the land which the Lord your God is giving you . . ." and still manages to say a lot with few words. This is something that is even obvious in our times. Capitalism cannot succeed in countries that do not have laws that protect the people. Capitalism is built on trust and a legal system that does not allow one's assets to be taken away illegally. Countries in which it is easy for government to seize the assets of people find that the wealth of its citizens flows to other countries. Micah (6:8) reduced the obligations of humankind to three major principles: "What does the Lord require of you: only to do justice, to love acts of kindness, and to walk discreetly before your God."

"'O my son Absalom, my son, my son Absalom! If only I had died instead of you! O Absalom, my son, my son!'" David's cry of torment at the death of his son is rendered in Hebrew using only 13 words, and only seven of them are distinct (II Samuel 19:1). He repeats the Hebrew word for "my son" eight times. This succinct cry of a parent carries within it a powerful and overwhelming passion. Absalom had rebelled against his father, King David, and tried to kill him. Despite all this, a parent's love does not ever go away. David may also have been crying to some extent because of his own feelings of guilt. David had been "angry" when Absalom's sister Tamar was raped by Amnon, David's son from another wife, but David did not punish Amnon (see II Samuel 13) and he realized that his injustice towards Tamar may have caused Absalom's rebellion. There are really no words that do justice to a parent's anguish but, if there were, it would be these.

Several powerful Biblical statements characterized by their brevity are simple—but not simplistic—adages or proverbs. From Psalms (146:3): "Put not your trust in princes, nor in the son of man, in whom there is no help." This verse, of course, emphasizes that we can only rely on God. Similarly, also in Psalms (31:1), we have: "In you, O Lord, do I put my trust; let me never be ashamed: deliver me in your righteousness." Another proverb (Proverbs 12:1) states: "Whoever loves correction loves knowledge, but he that hates criticism is a fool." The term used for fool (*baor*) actually means a boor or brute. A person who hates criticism and is unwilling to improve remains foolish and is compared to a brutish beast. Also from Proverbs (17:1): "Better a dry crust of bread with peace and quiet than a house full of contentious feasting." We often believe that those that have great wealth are much happier than the rest of us. A poor family that lives in peace and tranquility is often better off than the wealthiest households where everyone is fighting and miserable.

When Solomon was offered the Heavenly gift of anything his heart desired, he responded (I Kings 3:9): "Give therefore your servant an understanding heart to judge Your people, that I may discern between good and bad . . ." This is what Solomon asked of God. The most important value for a leader is to have an understanding heart, i.e., the wisdom to do the right thing. Leadership is not about acquiring wealth and power; it is about helping followers achieve their potential.

**Language**

When the language is what makes a verse resonate, it may be due to powerful imagery, to poetry, to a passionate turn of phrase. Sometimes the power of the message depends upon the poetry with which individual words are laced together to form the whole. Unfortunately, that doesn't always come through the process of translation from one language to another. The Russian poet Yevgeny Yevtushenko once remarked, in his restating of a French proverb, that "Translations are like women. When they are faithful they are not beautiful, and when they are beautiful they are not faithful." With that caveat, the following are some passages that resonate—certainly in Hebrew but, often, even in translation—because of the way the language is used in the service of the message contained within.

The most eloquent passage of all Scriptures may be the one spoken by Ruth to her mother-in-law, Naomi (Ruth 1:16-17):

> *Do not urge me to leave you or turn back from you. For wherever you go, I will go; wherever you live, I will live; your people will be my people and your God will be my God. Where you die, I will die, and there I will be buried.*

There is nothing more eloquent in all of literature than this statement showing Ruth's love for Naomi. At this point in the story Ruth's husband, Naomi's son, has died and both women are very poor. Ruth leaves her country Moab, her family and the pagan life to join the people of Israel.

The following passage from I Samuel (2:6-8) is part of Hannah's song. Hannah had been barren and then, when she gave birth to Samuel, she composed this prayer as gratitude to God.

> *The Lord brings death and gives life; he brings down to the grave and raises up. The Lord makes poor and makes rich; he humbles and he exalts. He raises up the poor from the dirt; he lifts the needy from the ash heap to make them sit with princes and endow them with a seat of honor. For the pillars of the earth are the Lord's, and on them he has set the world.*

This song is a message to all of us never to give up and at the same time hints that successful individuals should also be aware how easy it is to lose everything.

Some of the most powerful statements in Scriptures use memorable imagery and allegories to make important points. For example, the following passage from Isaiah (1:21-22):

> *How the faithful city has become a harlot! Once it was full of justice and righteousness lodged in it, but now—murderers! Your silver has become dross, your wine diluted with water. Your rulers are rebels and associates of thieves; each of them loves a bribe and chases after rewards.*

No prophet was more eloquent than Isaiah. This verse should be mandatory reading for all CEOs and politicians. The Great Recession of 2008 demonstrated how easy it was for the financial industry to destroy the economy and their own credibility with the public in order to enrich themselves. Politicians who have sold their souls to the lobbyists should have no difficulty understanding the verse: "Your rulers are . . . associates of thieves."

The imagery in the following famous passage is universally known (Isaiah 11: 6-9):

> *The wolf will live with the lamb, the leopard will lie down with the goat; the calf, the lion cub, and the fatling [will feed] together, and a small child will lead them. A cow and bear will graze together and their young will lie down together. The lion will eat straw like the cattle. An infant will play over a viper's hole, and a newly weaned child will stretch forth his hand over an adder's den. They will do no harm or damage anywhere in all of My holy mountain; for the earth will be filled with knowledge of God, as water covers the sea.*

This resounding message of world peace is still of great value today. It is a goal for humankind to strive towards. And here is another message of hope from Isaiah:

> *He gives power to the weak, and to those who have no might, He increases strength. Even youths grow tired and weary, and young men stumble and fall. But those who hope in God will renew their strength. They will soar on wings like eagles; they will run and not grow weary, they will walk and not be faint.*

This is Isaiah's (40:29-31) message of hope to those who have faith. This is reminiscent of the verse in Zechariah (4:6): "This is the word of God to Zerubbabel: 'Not by might, nor by power, but by My spirit,' says the Lord of Hosts."

"Let justice roll down as waters and righteousness as a mighty stream." This powerful verse from the prophet Amos (5:24) was used by the Reverend Martin Luther King, Jr. in his classic "I Have a Dream Speech" which Lucas and Medhurst (2012) consider to be "the most significant American political speech of the 20th century." Reverend King said:

> *We cannot be satisfied as long as a Negro in Mississippi cannot vote and a Negro in New York believes he has nothing for which to vote. No, no, we are not satisfied, and we will not be satisfied until 'justice rolls down like waters, and righteousness like a mighty stream.'*

In Lamentations (1:1), Jeremiah compares Jerusalem to a widow, alone and abandoned: "Alas, how does the city sit in solitude! The city that was great with people has become as a widow! She that was the greatest among nations, and princess among provinces, how is she become a tributary!" The prophet Jeremiah wonders how a great city such as Jerusalem has become so desolate and miserable. Of course, he knows the answer. This was divine retribution for their sins. Numerous prophets warned ancient Israel that this fate would befall them if they continued with their transgressions. This is a message to all countries that believe they can ignore the needs of the helpless and will remain powerful. In a similar vein (Lamentations 1:16), "For these things I weep; my eye, my eye runs down with water, because a comforter to relieve my soul is far from me: my children are forlorn, because the enemy has prevailed." The comforter (God) was far but he was definitely there watching. Indeed, 70 years later, the Jewish people returned to rebuild the Second Temple.

From Proverbs 6:6: "Go to the ant, you sluggard; observe her ways and be wise." According to Scripture, hard work and industriousness are very desirable qualities. The importance of productivity can be learned by observing the lowly ant. Both government and business play an important role in making sure that there is work for people. The verse in Proverbs (22:29) states: "Do you see a man diligent in his work? He will stand before kings; he will not stand before insignificant men." There is more about industriousness in the section which examines the content of these messages.

In the Book of Esther (4:14), Mordechai explains to Esther that leadership is about taking a chance in order to help the people: "For if you remain silent at this time, relief and deliverance will arise for the Jews from another place and you and your father's house will perish. And who knows whether you have not attained royalty for such a time as this?" Esther does risk her life and ends up saving all her people. She tells the king (8:6): "For how can I bear to see the calamity that will befall my people? How can I bear to see the destruction of my kindred?" A leader has to ensure that nothing bad happens to the people. The same can be said of CEOs; they have to make sure that they do not take risks that can endanger the jobs of employees solely to increase their bonuses. In the Book of Esther, even more than the language relaying the message, the very structure of the storyline does so. Individuals who were on top as the story opens are by the time the story ends, brought low by their own actions; and, vice versa. The message throughout is we reap what we sow, and just because we are on top (or on the bottom) now, it doesn't mean [we] can't fall (or rise) in the future.

**Content**

Sometimes it really is simply all about the message, rather than the medium or the delivery. Some of the more resonant and powerful—and highly cited—statements in the Bible have timeless messages such as industriousness, justice, integrity, compassion for the disenfranchised and for the less powerful members of society, redemption, and hope for a better tomorrow.

"When you shall eat of the toil of your hands, you will be happy and it will be well with you." This verse in Psalms (128:2) is just one of many that stress the importance of industriousness. Modern happiness research indicates that losing one's job has a huge impact on one's happiness; conversely, a good job contributes a great deal to one's happiness.

The "Woman of Valor" hymn in Proverbs (31:10-31) describes the attributes of the perfect wife.

> *She seeks out wool and flax, and works with her hands willingly. . . . She arises while it is yet night, and gives food to her household and a portion to her maidservants. She considers a field and buys it; from the fruit of her handiwork she plants a vineyard. . . . She knows that her merchandise is good. . . . She stretches out her hands onto the distaff, and her palms support the spindle. She spreads out her palm to the poor; and extends her hand to the needy. . . . She makes a cloak and sells it, and supplies aprons to the merchant. . . . She opens her mouth with wisdom; the lesson of kindness is on her tongue. . . . She does not eat the bread of idleness.*

What is fascinating about it is that it describes an entrepreneurial woman. The following are the traits of this ideal woman: she is industrious, entrepreneurial, honest, wise, and charitable. She cares for her entire household but also for the needy.

Exodus 20: 14: "You shall not covet your neighbor's house. You shall not covet your neighbor's wife, or his manservant or maidservant, his ox or donkey, or anything that belongs to your neighbor." This is the last of the 10 commandments, but in one way it is the most powerful of them. Individuals who are envious of others will never be satisfied. Moreover, they will often commit crimes such as robbery or murder to satisfy their needs. Research on happiness supports the view that the key to happiness is being satisfied with what you have and not focusing on what you do not have. Once a person gets on the "hedonic treadmill" and continues to demand more and more, not only will s/he never be satisfied but will also be tempted to do immoral and illegal acts.

"Who may abide in Your tent? Who may dwell on Your holy mountain? One who walks in total integrity, works righteously, and speaks truth in his heart." Here the Psalmist (Psalms 15:1-2) is providing us with what religion is truly about: helping others and being an upright, honest individual. Zechariah was also concerned with truth and honesty in business and declared (8:16-17): "Speak the truth every man with his fellow; with truth, justice and peace, judge in your gates. And let none of you contrive evil in your hearts against one another . . ."

Malachi (2:10) stated: "Have we not all one father? Has not one God created us? Why do we deal treacherously every man against his brother . . . ?" Indeed, the Bible tells us that all men are created equal. This is a powerful statement of the importance of every individual. Similarly, "Behold, how good and pleasant it is when brethren dwell together in unity." This verse from Psalms (133:1) is a simple plea for tolerance and diversity. We are all brothers, since all of us are descended from Adam and Eve. There is nothing more joyful than peace among all of humankind.

A pervasive message in Scriptures is that people should model themselves after God (i.e., *imitatio dei*) in the traits he values, such as justice and compassion. From Leviticus (19:2): "You shall be holy because I, the Lord your God, am holy." The idea of being holy and not doing anything which is an abomination to the Lord (e.g., false weights and measures) is repeated often in the Bible. It basically asks humankind to reject a selfish, atavistic life style and, instead, be a spiritual, caring person. From Leviticus 19:18: "Thou shalt love thy neighbor as thyself. I am the Lord." The Golden Rule is a foundation of every religion. Both Hillel and Confucius reworded this slightly so we also have the negative version of it: "What is hateful to you, do not do unto others."

The Bible tells us no fewer than 36 times to treat the stranger well. For example (Leviticus 19:34): "You shall treat the stranger who dwells with you as the native among you, and you shall love him as yourself, for you were strangers in the land of Egypt: I am the Lord your God." Societies that care about the rights of strangers thrive. America became great because it allowed immigrants from all over the world to come to this country. Try to imagine an America with only immigrants from England or from France or from Spain. Countries that have two classes of citizens often find themselves at war; civil wars are usually the most destructive of wars. The idea of "one law" for the citizen and stranger is repeated numerous times in the Bible. The idea that there should be one law for both the stranger and native is mentioned several times in the Bible. Thus, the Bible (Numbers 15: 16) states: "There is to be one law and one ordinance for you and the stranger that sojourns with you." Leviticus (25: 23) also states: "The land is mine, for you are strangers and settlers with me." This verse succinctly states what people always have to remember. The time we spend on Planet Earth is quite limited and everything we possess has to be left behind. All that we actually truly possess is our deeds. The good and bad that we do on this planet lives on after us.

From Zechariah (8:16): "These are the things which you should do: speak the truth to one another; judge with truth, justice, and peace in your gates." Without justice there can be no peace. And from Psalms (82:3-5): "Give justice for the poor and orphan; uphold the rights of the afflicted and the destitute. Rescue the poor and needy; deliver them from the hand of the wicked." The world cannot exist without justice and equity for all.

"Behold, this was the sin of your sister Sodom: She and her daughters had pride, plenty of bread, and untroubled tranquility; yet she did not strengthen the hand of the poor and the needy."

This verse (Ezekiel 16:49) teaches us that a country (or company) that does not care about the poor and needy does not deserve to survive. This is similar to Micah (3: 9-12):

> *Listen to my message, you leaders of the House of Jacob, you chiefs of the House of Israel, who abhor justice and who twist all that is straight, who build Zion with blood and Jerusalem with iniquity. Her leaders judge for bribes and her priests give rulings for a fee, and her prophets divine for pay. . . . Therefore, because of you, Zion shall be plowed over as a field; Jerusalem shall become a heap of rubble and the Temple Mount will become like a stone heap in the forest.*

Also from Micah (6:8): "He has told you, O man, what is good; and what does the Lord require of you, but to do justice, and to love kindness, and to walk humbly with your God?" We see here that justice and compassion must often go hand-in-hand.

The prophet Amos (8: 5-6) was concerned with various ways the poor were exploited by business such as hoarding food in order to resell it at exorbitant prices, tampering with weights and measures, and raising prices unjustly:

> *Listen to this, you who devour the needy, annihilating the poor of the land, saying when will the month pass, so that we can sell grain; the Sabbatical year, so that we can open the stores of grain; using an ephah that is too small and a shekel that is too large, and distorting dishonest scales. To purchase the poor with silver and the destitute for shoes, and selling the refuse of grain as grain.*

Hosea 2: 21-22: "I will betroth you to Me forever; and I will betroth you to Me in righteousness and in justice, in lovingkindness, and in compassion. I will betroth you to Me in faithfulness and you shall know the Lord." This is clearly a message of hope. Eventually all of humankind will recognize God and He will never again abandon His people. This is a beautiful and passionate analogy of the relationship between God and humankind. We are not simply serving a willful and/or vengeful God, but we are tied to God by characteristics and behavior expected. Once again, we return to the message of *imitatio dei*.

"Be strong and courageous. Do not be afraid or terrified because of them, for the Lord your God goes with you; He will never leave you nor forsake you." This verse from Deuteronomy (31:6) is reminiscent of Psalms 23: ". . . I will fear no evil, for you are with me. . . ." More of the verse from Psalms is referenced later in this paper in the next section. This verse could be the credo of all whistleblowers.

Hope and redemption are important messages as well. From Deuteronomy (30:4): "Even if your dispersed will be at the farthest parts of heaven, from there the Lord, your God, will gather you and from there He will bring you back." Once the people repent of their wicked ways, God will redeem them and bring them back from exile. The complete passage (verses 1-10) shows what will happen if the people repent. Another message of hope and redemption is found in Ezekiel (18:31-32): "Cast off from upon you all the transgressions that you have committed, and make yourselves a new heart and a new spirit. Why should you die, O House of Israel? For I have no pleasure in the death of anyone who dies, declares the Lord God. Therefore, repent and live!" This is another exhortation to repent and thus start afresh as though with a new heart and new spirit.

**Conclusion**

This paper examined a small selection of powerful statements from the Hebrew Bible. The ancient messages resonate today as much as they did thousands of years ago. The wolf will not lie down with the lamb until righteousness rolls down on humankind as a mighty stream. One Biblical message that has been used by many groups is "No justice, no peace" or "No peace without justice." This has been used to justify riots as well as peaceful demonstrations. Pope John Paul II (2002) spoke about this topic on the World Day of Peace. He quoted Isaiah (32: 17), and observed that "true peace is the work of justice." The complete quote is: "And the work of *tzedaka* (translated as either righteousness or justice) will be peace; and the effect of *tzedaka*, quietness and security forever." World peace cannot be possible without justice and equity for all.

Emma Lazarus (1849-1887), a Sephardic Jew, was an early advocate for an independent Jewish country in Palestine. She was also concerned about the plight of disenfranchised immigrants. She died at the young age of 38, but one line from her most famous poem, "The New Colossus," is strikingly Bible-like and will never be forgotten (Lyden, 2006): "Give me your tired, your poor, Your huddled masses yearning to breathe free. . . ."

These messages are meant for any people who seek meaning in their life. It is also hoped that individuals in leadership positions will use them as a guide for effective communication as well as a touchstone in understanding what truly is important.

*International Journal of Education and Research*, 1:2 (February 2013)
Reprinted with permission of the authors

# ARE YOU BEING AGGRESSIVE?
## 12 SIGNS OF AGGRESSION YOU NEED TO RECOGNISE

BY CARTHAGE BUCKLEY

You probably think of aggression in its most violent form i.e. shouting matches and fights. Aggression actually refers to any time that you try to get your own way without any regard for others. There are varying levels of aggression. Sometimes, it may be easy to spot aggression but quite often it is more subtle, manipulative and exploitative. When dealing with somebody who is being aggressive, the first step is to be able to recognise the aggression. The ability to recognise aggression is also essential from your own standpoint. There will be times, during discussion, when you become overheated and start to display signs of aggression. If you recognize this behaviour early, you can calm yourself down and adopt a more assertive approach before any real harm is done.

**Twelve Signs of Aggression**

The following are common signs of aggression. Not all of these signs will be displayed by each aggressive individual but familiarizing yourself with these signs will allow you to recognize the aggression quickly, and adjust your behaviour accordingly.

**1. It's all about what they want or need**

Aggressive people focus on themselves. Their wants and needs are all that matter and others do not get a look in. You will hear phrases such as:

Examples include:

- 'I want …'
- 'I need …'
- 'I must have …'

**CARTHAGE BUCKLEY**

Carthage Buckley is a stress and performance coach and the founder of *coachingpositiveperformance.com*. He holds a B.A. in accounting and human resource management from the National College of Ireland, and a M.Ed. in the psychology of education from the University of Bristol.

**2. It's all about how it affects them**

When something goes wrong, or when considering potential consequences, aggressive people only consider how it impacts upon them. The impact on others is irrelevant to them. As if that's not bad enough, if something has negative consequences for them, everybody else is expected to suffer the consequences too, e.g., I once knew a girl who, every time she had a row with her boyfriend, used to wake her entire family up so she could tell them how she had been unjustly treated.

It may seem like an extreme example but aggressive people will often attempt to turn their problem into everybody's problem.

**3. Unwillingness to accept responsibility**

Aggressive people rarely accept responsibility for the consequences they experience. There is usually someone else to be blamed. Assertive people look at a situation and attempt to identify areas where they can take responsibility and implement effective solutions. Aggressive people just look for ways to blame others so that they do not have to take any responsibility.

Examples include:

- 'I insulted John because he made me angry.'
- 'I was late because traffic was terrible' (ignoring the fact that traffic is always terrible and he didn't leave until the last minute)
- 'I asked John to do that for me. He's clearly not up to the job.'

Occasionally, it may be appropriate to highlight how mistakes made by others contributed to a problem but you will find that aggressive people turn blaming others into an art form. They see admission of responsibility as a weakness so they go on the defensive.

**4. They believe their opinion is fact**

For assertive communication to take place, it is important to be able to differentiate between opinion and facts. You may offer a suggestion or thoughts on something which has happened. In most circumstances, this should be fine. Aggressive people take it one step further. They assert their opinion as fact which is telling others that their opinions are irrelevant:

Examples include:

- 'This is what went wrong …'
- 'This is what we have to do …'
- 'That won't work …'
- 'That is/was stupid …'

**5. Aggressive enquiries**

When making inquiries or requests of others, it is best to approach them with an openness which invites them to offer their view. Aggressive people use their aggressive behaviour to close off that avenue before the other person gets a chance to respond. Aggressive questions are usually short, to the point and asked with a strong tone of voice:

Examples include:

- 'What do you think you are doing?'
- 'Why did you do that?'

Some of these aggressive questions can be difficult to recognize. If asked in the middle of a conversation, they may be useful questions. However, if asked at the beginning of the conversation, their purpose is to control the conversation and prevent the other person from offering their view.

**6. Aggressive demands**

Aggressive demands occur when every opportunity is made to prevent the other person from declining the request. This is often done via threats:

Examples include:

- 'If you do not do this …'
- 'You need to do this or …'

You also need to beware of the people who are a little more subtle with their demands, e.g., those who appear to ask a favour but walk away before you respond. These people are not giving you the opportunity to decline. This is a more subtle form of aggression.

**7. Undermining**

Some aggressive people resort to undermining others to make themselves look better by comparison. There are many ways to undermine but they usually involve either putting the other person into a difficult position in order to highlight a weakness or ridicule them; or, they often use subtle tactics to suggest that the person is not up to the job. Their aim is to erode other people's confidence in the individual they are undermining. If they can erode that person's confidence in themselves, they may see that as a bonus.

Examples include:

- Pulling out of a presentation/meeting at the last minute and leaving the other person to deliver it unprepared.
- Rather than ask a subordinate if they have completed their work, the manager emails all of the people they carry out work for to ask if the work has been completed.
- Asking others to perform tasks for which they are not suitable and failing to provide the necessary support.

**8. Manipulative Advice Giving**

In reality, this is not advice giving. This is telling people what to do and attempting to disguise it as advice. The recipient is not expected to disagree or voice an opinion. They are expected to follow the "advice" and be grateful for it:

Examples include:

- 'If I were you …'
- 'The best thing for you to do would be …'

**9. Rapid speech**

Aggressive people speak fast with little or no pauses. They are determined to get their point across and have no desire to let the other person offer their input. They want total control of the conversation and are determined that the other person will hear what they have to say.

**10. Loud voice with emphasized blame**

Aggressive people are determined to be heard. They wish to send a clear signal to others that they are speaking and they will not be talked over or talked down. Although already loud, they tend to place extra emphasis on the parts of their speech where they place the blame on others.

**11. Aggressive talking; defensive listening**

This refers to the body language that they adopt during their bout of aggression. When talking they will likely lean forward. They may point, remonstrate, gesticulate etc. However, when the other person is speaking they will adopt a more defensive posture, e.g., crossing their arms.

**12. Intense eye contact**

If you cannot work out whether someone is staring at you, or staring through you, you are looking at someone who is full of aggression. At that moment in time, they believe that you are the source of all of their problems. They are in fight mode, and in fight mode you don't take your eyes off of your opponent.

The best way to overcome aggression, whether it is you or somebody else who is the aggressor, is to learn to identify and understand the causes of your aggression. This can be followed with effective anger management techniques.

Communication and interpersonal relationships work best when both parties come together from a position of respect and attempt to find workable solutions which meet the needs of both parties. While it is not always possible to meet the needs of both parties, starting off seeking mutual benefit makes it easier to achieve an acceptable compromise. Aggression ignores this approach. Aggression occurs when one party has no regard for the other. They are only concerned with having their own needs met and have little concern for how that might affect others. Aggression is a source of unnecessary conflict and causes lasting damage to relationships. Being familiar with the signs of aggressive behaviour will help you to recognize when you, or someone whom you are in discussion with, is being aggressive. You will then be able to adjust your behaviour to manage the situation more appropriately and to prevent unnecessary conflict.

www.coachingpositiveperformance.com
Reprinted with permission of the author

## HAVE SOMETHING IMPORTANT TO SAY?
## CONVERSATION TIPS FROM SINAI

BY RABBI NAFTALI SILBERBERG

What's the difference between speaking and nagging? Speech involves one individual speaking words and ideas, another individual hearing words and ideas. Nagging is defined as one person articulating words and thoughts, another person hearing—at best—grating static.

**RABBI NAFTALI SILBERBERG**

Rabbi Naftali Silberberg, a noted author and lecturer, is the co-director of curriculum for the Rohr Jewish Learning Institute and co-editor in chief of its Flagship division.

We usually have only one chance to communicate an important message. If we botch that opportunity, the odds of the recipient "getting" the message in a second go-round are greatly minimized. As such, substantial thought and planning should precede any conversation of significance.

In our nation's 3,300 year history, G-d has directly addressed us exactly once, when G-d descended upon Mount Sinai and gave ten commandments to an assembled nation. One communiqué that was intended to last more than three millennia. Without a doubt, the Creator of speech utilized this opportunity to its maximum, and assured that the words He uttered would enter one ear—and then stay put.

The Midrash says that the mighty voice that spoke the Ten Commandments had no echo. An echo occurs when sound waves encounter resistance, striking an impenetrable obstruction. G-d's voice had no echo because it penetrated. It pierced desert mountains and human minds and hearts—nothing and no one blocked the voice out.

In doing so, G-d also left us a perfect prototype to follow on those occasions when we really want our words to be taken seriously.

Here are some conversation lessons I gleaned from the Great Communication:

**Don't "btw" It**

It wasn't sudden or unexpected. It wasn't "Oh, good that you're here. There's something I wanted to discuss . . ." or "*What* did you just do? We've got to have a talk *right* now!"

Three days in advance G-d relayed to the Israelites that He had an important message. When the time arrived, the nation was prepared, curious, and eager. The momentousness of the occasion had sunk in—and they were receptive.

**Choose Your Timing**

*"On the third day when it was becoming morning . . ."* Considering that the Sinai event featured a spectacular "light and sound" show ("And all the people could see the sound and the flames"), would it not have been that more impressive and awe-inspiring had the event been scheduled for after dark?

Apparently G-d did not want to address a weary nation. He chose a moment when the mind is clear and most alert—and receptive.

**Choose Your Setting**

*"When G-d gave the Torah, a bird did not chirp or take wing, an ox didn't low, angels didn't fly or sing G-d's praise, the sea didn't move . . ." (Midrash).* Contrary to popular conception, the Talmud tells us that G-d is not in the habit of performing miracles simply to impress. Every miracle has a purpose. So why did G-d hush all other voices aside for His own? Would His voice have been drowned out by all this common background noise? Or is the elimination of even minor distractions vital to creating an atmosphere wherein the listener is completely tuned in and receptive?

**Use Both Sides of Your Mouth**

The Midrash also tells us that G-d's voice serenaded the Israelites from all four directions, as well as from above and below. Before delivering your message, ask yourself: "Am I broadcasting this message from all directions? Or is there some part of me that is signaling a different message altogether?" If that is the case, have a conversation with yourself before attempting to convince another. If you have not internalized the message, there's little chance that you will find the other person receptive.

**Mince Words**

The whole grandiose event centered around ten commandments, expressed in exactly 620 letters. It left room for the addressees to ponder the words and consider its multiple meanings and lessons. It gave room for thought instead of stifling it. Got the other person to think? He's already receptive!

# *Lesson* 4

A Young Scholar and His Tutor, *Rembrandt Harmenszoon van Rijn, oil on canvas, c. 1630. (The J. Paul Getty Museum, Los Angeles)*

## LEADING WORDS

### THE ART OF INSPIRATION AND INFLUENCE

"A leader takes people where they want to go. A great leader takes people where they don't necessarily want to go, but ought to be."

—Rosalynn Carter

*At times, it is necessary to influence, guide, teach, or correct others—often taking people where they ought to be. This lesson leans on the insights of the Jewish sages to discover how to influence, the responsibilities involved, the means of measuring success, the ability to recognize a communicator projecting personal insecurities on others in a failed attempt to communicate, and the preeminence of motivation over technique.*

# Exercise 1

How many communication gaffes can you detect in the exchange depicted in the video?

| | |
|---|---|
| 1 | |
| 2 | |
| 3 | |
| 4 | |
| 5 | |

# Exercise 2

If you were granted the supernatural power of unlimited influence on your fellow humans, what would you do with this power?

In your family life:

In your business or social life:

In society at large:

# TEXT 1

PSALMS 47:4

יַדְבֵּר עַמִּים תַּחְתֵּינוּ.

God brings nations under our leadership.

The Maggid, *Zalman Kleinman, watercolor on paper, 1981.*

# Figure 4.1

Speech and Leadership

| יַדְבֵּר | יְדַבֵּר | דַּבָּר | דַּבֵּר |
|---|---|---|---|
| Leadership | Speech | Leader | Speak |

# TEXT 2

NIRAJ CHOKSHI, "TEENAGERS RECORDED A DROWNING MAN AND LAUGHED," *THE NEW YORK TIMES,* JULY 21, 2017

The video was shocking in Florida, where shocking videos seem like a genre. A group of teenagers laughed and watched [and recorded video] as a man struggled in the water of a pond. The man drowned, and his body was not found for days.

The five teenagers did nothing to help him, not even call 911, but after examining the video, the authorities said this week that they did not break the law. "In the state of Florida, there is no law in place that requires a person to render aid or call to render aid to a victim in distress," Yvonne Martinez, a spokeswoman for the Cocoa Police Department, said on Friday. . . .

The man, Jamel Dunn, 31, drowned July 9, and his body was found five days later. . . . The low-quality, 2.5-minute cellphone video was provided to The New York Times by [the state attorney for Brevard and Seminole Counties's] office and earlier obtained by Florida Today. It shows a man flailing in the middle of a body of water as the teenagers describe his struggle and laugh at him from the shore.

# TEXT 3

MAIMONIDES, *MISHNEH TORAH*, LAWS OF MURDER AND SAFEGUARDING OF LIFE 1:14

כָּל הַיָּכוֹל לְהַצִּיל וְלֹא הִצִּיל, עוֹבֵר עַל "לֹא תַעֲמֹד עַל דַּם רֵעֶךָ" (וַיִּקְרָא יט, טז).

וְכֵן הָרוֹאֶה אֶת חֲבֵרוֹ טוֹבֵעַ בַּיָּם, אוֹ לִסְטִים בָּאִים עָלָיו, אוֹ חַיָּה רָעָה בָּאָה עָלָיו, וְיָכוֹל לְהַצִּילוֹ הוּא בְּעַצְמוֹ, אוֹ שֶׁיִּשְׂכֹּר אֲחֵרִים לְהַצִּילוֹ, וְלֹא הִצִּיל.

A person who can save a fellow [who is being threatened with murder] but fails to do so is in violation of the injunction: "Do not stand idly by [the shedding of] your fellow's blood" (LEVITICUS 19:16).

Similarly, one is in violation of "Do not stand idly by your fellow's blood" if one sees someone drowning at sea or being attacked by robbers or a wild animal, and is in a position to save him or her, or to hire others to do so, but refrains from assisting.

**RABBI MOSHE BEN MAIMON (MAIMONIDES, RAMBAM) 1135–1204**

Halachist, philosopher, author, and physician. Maimonides was born in Córdoba, Spain. After the conquest of Córdoba by the Almohads, he fled Spain and eventually settled in Cairo, Egypt. There, he became the leader of the Jewish community and served as court physician to the vizier of Egypt. He is most noted for authoring the *Mishneh Torah*, an encyclopedic arrangement of Jewish law, and for his philosophical work, *Guide for the Perplexed*. His rulings on Jewish law are integral to the formation of halachic consensus.

# TEXT 4

MAIMONIDES, *SEFER HAMITZVOT*, POSITIVE MITZVAH 205

> וְאַל יֹאמַר אָדָם: "אֲנִי לֹא אֶחֱטָא. וְאִם יֶחֱטָא זוּלָתִי, זֶה עִנְיָינוֹ עִם ה'!" זֶה נֶגֶד הַתּוֹרָה. אֶלָּא אָנוּ מְצוּוִּים שֶׁלֹּא לַעֲבוֹר וְלֹא נַנִּיחַ לְזוּלָתֵנוּ מֵאֻמָּתֵנוּ לַעֲבוֹר.

One should not say, "I will act righteously, and if someone else chooses to stray from the path of righteousness, that is a matter that is between him and God." This attitude is inconsistent with Torah [values]. Rather, we are commanded to do the right thing ourselves, and to see to it that others, too, conduct themselves appropriately.

# TEXT 5

RABBI SHNE'UR ZALMAN OF LIADI, *TORAH OR* 4A

> וְעַל שֵׁם זֶה נִקְרָא מְדַבֵּר, מִלָּשׁוֹן "יַדְבֵּר עַמִּים", כְּלוֹמַר שֶׁהוּא הַמַּנְהִיג אֶת כּוּלָם, בִּהְיוֹתוֹ מַעֲלֶה אוֹתָם עַל יְדֵי עֲבוֹדָתוֹ.

The human being is called a *medaber* (an "articulating being"), which is related to the word *yadber* in the verse, "God brings nations under our leadership." The name *medaber* points to our calling to lead all of Creation and to elevate all that we encounter through our service of God.

**RABBI SHNE'UR ZALMAN OF LIADI (ALTER REBBE) 1745–1812**

Chasidic rebbe, halachic authority, and founder of the Chabad movement. The Alter Rebbe was born in Liozna, Belarus, and was among the principal students of the Magid of Mezeritch. His numerous works include the *Tanya*, an early classic containing the fundamentals of Chabad Chasidism, and *Shulchan Aruch HaRav*, an expanded and reworked code of Jewish law.

# TEXT 6

MIDRASH, *YALKUT SHIMONI* (WAGSHAL EDITION), VAYIKRA 471

שֶׁכָּל יִשְׂרָאֵל נִקְרְאוּ נֶפֶשׁ אַחַת . . . כּוּלָם עֲרֵבִים זֶה בָּזֶה.

לְמָה הַדָּבָר דּוֹמֶה? לִבְנֵי אָדָם שֶׁהָיוּ בָּאִין בִּסְפִינָה, נָטַל אֶחָד מַקְדֵּחַ וְהִתְחִיל קוֹדֵחַ תַּחְתָּיו. אָמְרוּ לוֹ: "שׁוֹטֶה! אַתָּה קוֹדֵחַ תַּחְתֶּיךָ, וְהַמַּיִם נִכְנָסִין וְכוּלָּן אֲבוּדִין!"

All of Israel is considered a single soul. . . . Each of us is responsible for every one of our fellows.

This can be compared to seafarers who were traveling on a boat. One of the boat's passengers took a drill and began to bore a hole in the hull beneath [his cabin]. His fellow passengers protested: "Fool! You may be drilling [only] beneath your [cabin]. But the water will flood the entire boat, and drown us all!"

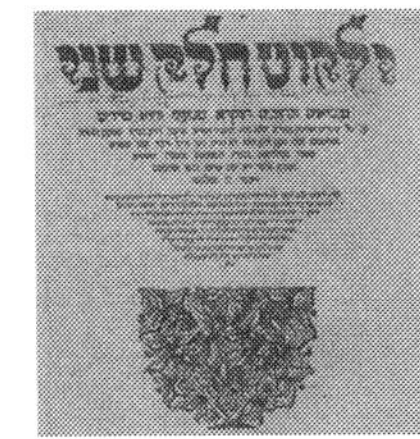

***YALKUT SHIMONI***

A Midrash that covers the entire biblical text. Its material is collected from all over rabbinic literature, including the Babylonian and Jerusalem Talmuds and various ancient Midrashic texts. It contains several passages from Midrashim that have been lost, as well as different versions of existing Midrashim. It is unclear when and by whom this Midrash was redacted.

Sailing Boat, *Adams Alksnis, 1897. (Latvian National Museum of Art, Riga)*

# TEXT 7

RABBI JOSEPH B. SOLOVEITCHIK, *YEMEI ZIKARON*, P. 11

הָאָדָם נִבְרָא בְּתוֹר שָׁלִיחַ. עֶצֶם הַיְצִירָה, הַלֵּידָה, מְכִילָה בְּתוֹכָהּ בְּהֶכְרֵחַ אֶת דְּבַר מִינּוּי הַשְּׁלִיחוּת. אֶת הָעוּבְדָה שֶׁמִּישֶׁהוּ חַי בִּזְמַן מְסוּיָּם, בִּתְקוּפָה מְיוּחֶדֶת, וּבְמָקוֹם מוּגְדָּר, וְלֹא נוֹלַד בִּתְקוּפָה אַחֶרֶת וּבְנְסִיבוֹת אֲחֵרוֹת, נוּכַל לְהָבִין אַךְ וְרַק אִם נְקַבֵּל אֶת עֶצֶם הָרַעְיוֹן בִּדְבַר שְׁלִיחוּתוֹ שֶׁל הָאָדָם.

שְׁלִיחוּתוֹ שֶׁל הַקָּדוֹשׁ בָּרוּךְ הוּא לָאָדָם הִיא בִּבְחִינַת דָּבָר שֶׁאֵינוֹ קָצוּב בִּזְמַן - הִיא שְׁלִיחוּת מַתְמֶדֶת. מִזְּמַן לִזְמַן מְקַבֵּל הָאָדָם תַּפְקִידִים וּמַעֲשִׂים חֲדָשִׁים. זוֹהִי שְׁלִיחוּת לְכָל הַחַיִּים, וְהִיא מִסְתַּיֶּימֶת עִם הַמָּוֶת.

We, human beings, are created as agents with a mission. The fact of our formation, our birth, indicates the assignment of a mission. The fact that someone was born at a certain time, in a particular era, and in a specific place—and was not born in a different era or under different circumstances—can be understood only if we accept the concept of human purpose.

The mission assigned by God is not limited to a specific time [in a person's lifetime], rather, it is continuous. From time to time, the human being will be assigned new roles and tasks. Our mission is lifelong and ends only with death.

**RABBI JOSEPH B. SOLOVEITCHIK**
**1903–1993**

Talmudist and philosopher. A scion of a famous Lithuanian rabbinical family, Rabbi Soloveitchik was one of the most influential Jewish personalities, leaders, and thinkers of the 20th century. In 1941, he became professor of Talmud at RIETS—Yeshiva University; in this capacity, he ordained more rabbis than anyone else in Jewish history. Among his published works are *Halakhic Man* and *Lonely Man of Faith*.

# TEXT 8

TALMUD, ARACHIN 16B

אָמַר רַבִּי טַרְפוֹן: "תָּמֵהַ אֲנִי אִם יֵשׁ בַּדּוֹר הַזֶּה שֶׁמְקַבֵּל תּוֹכָחָה. אִם אָמַר לוֹ, 'טוֹל קֵיסָם מִבֵּין שִׁינֶיךָ', אָמַר לוֹ 'טוֹל קוֹרָה מִבֵּין עֵינֶיךָ'".

אָמַר רַבִּי אֶלְעָזָר בֶּן עֲזַרְיָה: "תְּמִיהַנִי אִם יֵשׁ בַּדּוֹר הַזֶּה שֶׁיּוֹדֵעַ לְהוֹכִיחַ".

Rabbi Tarfon said: "I wonder if there is anyone in this generation who knows how to *accept* critique. For if one person chides another, the other responds, 'You are guilty of even greater indiscretions, [so how dare you reprove me for mine]?'"

Rabbi Elazar ben Azariah said: "I wonder if there is anyone in this generation who knows how to properly *give* critique."

**BABYLONIAN TALMUD**

A literary work of monumental proportions that draws upon the legal, spiritual, intellectual, ethical, and historical traditions of Judaism. The 37 tractates of the Babylonian Talmud contain the teachings of the Jewish sages from the period after the destruction of the 2nd Temple through the 5th century CE. It has served as the primary vehicle for the transmission of the Oral Law and the education of Jews over the centuries; it is the entry point for all subsequent legal, ethical, and theological Jewish scholarship.

## QUESTION FOR DISCUSSION

Why is it so difficult to accept critique?

# TEXT 9

LEVITICUS 19:17

לֹא תִשְׂנָא אֶת אָחִיךָ בִּלְבָבֶךָ; הוֹכֵחַ תּוֹכִיחַ אֶת עֲמִיתֶךָ.

Do not nurse hatred for your brother in your heart; you shall surely rebuke your fellow.

# TEXT 10

THE REBBE, RABBI MENACHEM MENDEL SCHNEERSON, *LIKUTEI SICHOT* 15:91

וֶוען אֵיינֶער אִיז מוֹכִיחַ אַ צְוֵוייטְן בְּלוֹיז צוּ מְקַיֵים זַיין דֶעם צִיווּי "הוֹכֵחַ תּוֹכִיחַ אֶת עֲמִיתֶךָ", אִיז אֲפִילוּ וֶוען עֶר טוּט עֶס "מֵאָה פְּעָמִים" ווִירְקְט עֶס נִיט אוֹיף יֶענֶעם אַזוֹי שְׁטַארְק ווִי אַ תּוֹכָחָה וָואס אִיז אוֹיסְן **יֶענֶעמ'ס** טוֹבָה.

וְיֵשׁ לוֹמַר, שֶׁזֶּהוּ גַּם הַטַּעַם מַה שֶׁתּוֹכַחְתּוֹ שֶׁל נֹחַ לֹא פָּעֲלָה עֲלֵיהֶם שֶׁיִּתְעוֹרְרוּ בִּתְשׁוּבָה.

If a person critiques another in order to fulfill the Torah's instruction, "Rebuke your neighbor," even if done repeatedly, it will not have the same effect as a critique that is motivated by sincere care for one's fellow.

Perhaps this is the reason why Noah's admonitions were ineffective and did not cause anyone to change their ways.

**RABBI MENACHEM MENDEL SCHNEERSON 1902–1994**

The towering Jewish leader of the 20th century, known as "the Lubavitcher Rebbe," or simply as "the Rebbe." Born in southern Ukraine, the Rebbe escaped Nazi-occupied Europe, arriving in the U.S. in June 1941. The Rebbe inspired and guided the revival of traditional Judaism after the European devastation, impacting virtually every Jewish community the world over. The Rebbe often emphasized that the performance of just one additional good deed could usher in the era of Mashiach. The Rebbe's scholarly talks and writings have been printed in more than 200 volumes.

# TEXT 11

THE REBBE, RABBI MENACHEM MENDEL SCHNEERSON,
*SEFER HASICHOT* 5751, 1:85–86

> נִיט נָאר וָואס בַּא דֶער אִשָּׁה אִיז נִיטָא קֵיין חִסָּרוֹן לְגַבֵּי הָאִישׁ, נָאר אַדְּרַבָּה: אִיר אוֹפֶן הַפְּעוּלָּה הָאט אִין זִיךְ אַ מַעֲלָה לְגַבֵּי פְּעוּלַּת הָאִישׁ: וְוִיבַּאלְד אַז "אִישׁ דַּרְכּוֹ לִכְבּוֹשׁ", בַּאוַוייְזְט עֶס אַז דֶער עִיקָּר אוֹפֶן וְוִי עֶר קֶען אוֹיפְטָאן אִיז דוּרְךְ כִּיבּוּשׁ וּמֶמְשָׁלָה (אוּן נִיט דוּרְךְ מַלְכוּתוֹ **בְּרָצוֹן** קִבְּלוּ עֲלֵיהֶם) ... מַה שֶּׁאֵין כֵּן אַן אִשָּׁה, וָואס "אֵין דַּרְכָּהּ לִכְבּוֹשׁ", טוּט אוֹיךְ בְּאוֹפֶן "פְּנִימָה", בְּכָבוֹד וּבְדֶרֶךְ אֶרֶץ (בְּאוֹפֶן שֶׁל "נַייחָא"), אַ הַשְׁפָּעָה פְּנִימִית - אַזוֹי אַז דֶעם מִיט וֶועמֶען מְ'טוּט אוֹיךְ זָאל מְקַבֵּל זַיין בְּרָצוֹן עַצְמוֹ דִי הַשְׁפָּעָה ...
>
> בִּיז אַז דֶער דֶּרֶךְ הָעֲבוֹדָה פוּן נְשֵׁי וּבְנוֹת יִשְׂרָאֵל, וֶוערְט אוֹיךְ אַ לִימוּד וּמוֹרֶה דֶּרֶךְ צוּ אֲנָשִׁים וּבָנִים וְוִי זֵיי דַארְפְן טָאן זֵייעֶר עֲבוֹדָה.

The Talmud (YEVAMOT 65A) says, "It is the way of a man to conquer; it is not the way of a woman to conquer."

A woman's style of influence has a unique advantage over a man's. As a result of the masculine tendency to "conquer," the principal methods of male achievement are conquest and control, methods that do not evoke willful acceptance. . . . Women, by contrast, who are not naturally inclined to "conquer," have a deeper impact on others. Because the feminine approach is characterized by respect and congeniality, the recipients are transformed of their own volition. . . .

The approach of Jewish women and girls sets an example to be followed by men and boys.

# TEXT 12

GENESIS 9:20–23

וַיָּחֶל נֹחַ אִישׁ הָאֲדָמָה וַיִּטַּע כָּרֶם. וַיֵּשְׁתְּ מִן הַיַּיִן וַיִּשְׁכָּר, וַיִּתְגַּל בְּתוֹךְ אָהֳלֹה. וַיַּרְא חָם אֲבִי כְנַעַן אֵת עֶרְוַת אָבִיו, וַיַּגֵּד לִשְׁנֵי אֶחָיו בַּחוּץ.

וַיִּקַּח שֵׁם וָיֶפֶת אֶת הַשִּׂמְלָה וַיָּשִׂימוּ עַל שְׁכֶם שְׁנֵיהֶם וַיֵּלְכוּ אֲחֹרַנִּית, וַיְכַסּוּ אֵת עֶרְוַת אֲבִיהֶם, וּפְנֵיהֶם אֲחֹרַנִּית וְעֶרְוַת אֲבִיהֶם לֹא רָאוּ.

Noah started farming and he planted a vineyard. He drank of the wine and became drunk, and he [lay] naked in his tent. Ham, the father of Canaan, saw his father's nakedness, and he reported this to his two brothers outside.

Shem and Japheth took the garment, they placed it on both of their shoulders as they walked backward, and they covered their father's nakedness. Their faces were turned backward, and they did not see their father's nakedness.

Noah's Ark *(detail), Reb Shalom of Safed (1896–1980). (Smith College Museum of Art, Massachusetts)*

## Figure 4.2

Attitude Checklist

Before attempting to offer someone constructive critique, ensure that:

- You are motivated only by your concern for your fellow.
- You do not seek to control your fellow.
- You are not in any way judging or condemning your fellow.

# Figure 4.3

H.A.L.T.

Before entering into a sensitive conversation, check to see whether either you, or your conversation partner, are:

- Hungry
- Angry
- Lonely
- Tired

If yes, HALT!

# TEXT 13

TALMUD, YEVAMOT 65B

כְּשֵׁם שֶׁמִּצְוָה עַל אָדָם לוֹמַר דָּבָר הַנִּשְׁמָע, כָּךְ מִצְוָה עַל אָדָם שֶׁלֹּא לוֹמַר דָּבָר שֶׁאֵינוֹ נִשְׁמָע.

Just as it is a mitzvah to say words that will be accepted, it is a mitzvah *not* to say words if they will not be accepted.

# TEXT 14

MAIMONIDES, *MISHNEH TORAH*, LAWS OF CHARACTER DEVELOPMENT 6:7

הַמּוֹכִיחַ אֶת חֲבֵרוֹ - בֵּין בִּדְבָרִים שֶׁבֵּינוֹ לְבֵינוֹ בֵּין בִּדְבָרִים שֶׁבֵּינוֹ לְבֵין הַמָּקוֹם - צָרִיךְ לְהוֹכִיחוֹ בֵּינוֹ לְבֵין עַצְמוֹ, וִידַבֵּר לוֹ בְּנַחַת וּבְלָשׁוֹן רַכָּה, וְיוֹדִיעוֹ שֶׁאֵינוֹ אוֹמֵר לוֹ אֶלָּא לְטוֹבָתוֹ, וְלַהֲבִיאוֹ לְחַיֵּי הָעוֹלָם הַבָּא.

When we chastise a fellow—whether regarding an interpersonal issue or a moral matter—it should be done in private. We should deliver our words with patience and gentleness, and inform our fellow that we are only motivated by his or her welfare and our desire that he or she merit reward in the World to Come.

# TEXT 15a

PROVERBS 24:24–25

> אֹמֵר לְרָשָׁע, "צַדִּיק אָתָּה!"
> יִקְּבֻהוּ עַמִּים, יִזְעָמוּהוּ לְאֻמִּים.
>
> וְלַמּוֹכִיחִים יִנְעָם,
> וַעֲלֵיהֶם תָּבוֹא בִרְכַּת טוֹב.

He who says to a wicked man, "You are righteous," peoples will curse him, nations will abhor him.

It is pleasant, however, for those who rebuke the wicked; a good blessing will come upon them.

# TEXT 15b

RABBI MOSHE ALSHICH, *RAV PENINIM*, AD LOC.

וּלְעִנְיַן סְמִיכוּת הַכְּתוּבִים "אֹמֵר לְרָשָׁע כו'", "וְלַמּוֹכִיחִים וְכו'", שָׁמַעְתִּי בְּשֵׁם קַדְמוֹנִים שֶׁאָמַר:

"אוֹמֵר לְרָשָׁע, 'צַדִּיק אַתָּה', יִקְּבֻהוּ עַמִּים וְכו'", שֶׁיִּתְגָּאֶה הָרָשָׁע וְיִתְפַּקֵּר לַעֲשׂוֹת רַע גַּם אֶת הַכְּלָל בְּסִיבַּת הַמַּחֲזִיק בְּיָדוֹ.

אַךְ לְמוֹכִיחִים אֶת הָרְשָׁעִים לַהֲבִיאָם לְמוּטָב, יִנְעָם לָהֶם לֵאמֹר לְרָשָׁע, "צַדִּיק אַתָּה". לוֹמַר: "הֲלֹא צַדִּיק אַתָּה וּבֶן טוֹבִים, וְלֹא נַאֲמִין לְמַעֲבִירֵי הַקּוֹל עָלֶיךָ. לָכֵן אֱחוֹז צַדִּיק דֶּרֶךְ הַטּוֹבָה גָּלוּי לַכֹּל, לְמַעַן יִרְאוּ וְיֵבוֹשׁוּ וְיִסָּכְרוּ פִּי דוֹבְרֵי שֶׁקֶר".

וּבַעֲשׂוֹתָם כַּדָּבָר הַזֶּה, בְּמָקוֹם שֶׁלְּבִלְתִּי מוֹכִיחִים "יִקְּבֻהוּ עַמִּים וְכו'", עַל אֵלֶּה "תָּבֹא בִּרְכַּת טוֹב".

וְאֵין סָפֵק כִּי זֶה הוּא פְּשַׁט הַכָּתוּב בֶּאֱמֶת.

I've heard in the name of early sages the reason why these two verses are juxtaposed against each other:

People curse "he who says to a wicked man, 'You are righteous,'" because this praise fuels the wicked person's arrogance and causes him to do even greater evil.

However, "for those who rebuke the wicked" in an attempt to lead them back to the path of righteousness, "it is pleasant" to "say to a wicked man, 'You are righteous.'" It is pleasant to rebuke another by saying: "I don't believe a word of what is being said about you! You are, after all, a wonderful person and of upstanding upbringing. Show everyone just how good you are, so

**RABBI MOSHE ALSHICH**
**1508–1593**

Biblical exegete. Rabbi Alshich was born in Turkey and moved to Safed, Israel, where he became a student of Rabbi Yosef Caro, the preeminent codifier of Jewish law. Alshich's biblical, homiletical, and ethical teachings remain popular to this day, most notably, *Torat Moshe*, a commentary on the Torah. His students included Rabbi Chaim Vital and Rabbi Yom Tov Tsahalon. He is buried in Safed.

that those who speak badly of you will be ashamed and silenced." One who rebukes in this manner, instead of inducing curses and inviting abhorrence, is the recipient of "good blessings."

I have no doubt that this is the true interpretation of these verses.

The Reprimand, *Walters Shirlaw, etching, 1882. (The National Gallery of Art, Washington, D.C.)*

## Figure 4.4

Technique Checklist

When attempting to offer constructive critique, ensure that:

- You are in a private setting.
- Your demeanor, tone, and the content of your words are soft and gentle.
- You notify the recipient that you are motivated only by your concern for his or her welfare.
- You speak to the recipient's inherent goodness and infinite potential.

# TEXT 16

RABBI ELIEZER PAPO, *PELE YO'ETS, TOCHACHAH*

וְיוֹתֵר יִגְדַּל הַחִיּוּב עַל שְׁאָר עַמָּא, שֶׁדִּבְרֵיהֶם עוֹשִׂים פֵּירוֹת יוֹתֵר מִדִּבְרֵי הֶחָכָם, שֶׁאִם יוֹכִיחֶנּוּ הֶחָכָם, יֹאמְרוּ, "הוּא חָכָם, הוּא חָסִיד, וּמִי יוּכַל לַעֲשׂוֹת כְּמַעֲשֵׂהוּ? אִם הָיִינוּ כֻּלָּנוּ כְּמוֹתוֹ, הָיָה בָּא הַמָּשִׁיחַ!" כְּאִילּוּ בִּיאַת הַמָּשִׁיחַ הִיא דָּבָר בִּלְתִּי אֶפְשָׁר עַל יָדֵינוּ.

וְעוֹד, שֶׁהֶחָכָם אֵינוֹ מָצוּי תָּדִיר אֵצֶל עַמֵּי הָאָרֶץ וְאֵינוֹ רוֹאֶה בְּמַעֲשֵׂיהֶם, לֹא כֵּן חֲבֵרוֹ הָרָגִיל אֶצְלוֹ, וְכַאֲשֶׁר יוֹכִיחֵם וְיֹאמַר לָהֶם, "אַל נָא אַחַי תָּרֵעוּ, וְגַם לִי לֵבָב כְּמוֹכֶם לַעֲשׂוֹת כְּמַעֲשֵׂיכֶם, אַךְ חוֹשְׁשַׁנִי לִי מֵחַטָּאת"...

כָּזֹאת וְכָזֹאת יְדַבֵּר אִישׁ אֶל רֵעֵהוּ, וּדְבָרָיו עוֹשִׂים פֵּירוֹת.

The obligation [to strive to influence our fellows to improve their ways] applies especially to the laypeople, whose words yield greater results than those of scholars. For if a scholar reproves another, the person typically responds: "He is a scholar and a pious person—who can possibly emulate his ways? If we were all like him, the Messiah would have come already!" (As if people of our caliber cannot bring the Messiah on our own!)

Moreover, scholars don't frequent the same places as the common folk, and therefore are unaware of their actions. A close friend, on the other hand, can say: "Brother, please don't make this terrible mistake. I too would love to do the same as you, but I am loath to do that which is unethical." . . .

When one speaks words such as these to his fellow, they produce the desired results.

**RABBI ELIEZER PAPO**
**1785–1826**

Scholar and author. Born in Sarajevo, Rabbi Papo was an outstanding rabbinic scholar, noted for his piety and holiness. He served as rabbi of the community of Selestria (today in Bulgaria). In spite of his short life, Rabbi Papo achieved remarkable depth and breadth in his rabbinic scholarship, and left to posterity a significant literary legacy—most notably, his work *Pele Yo'ets*, on the topics of Jewish ethics, morals, and personality development.

## Exercise 3

In today's lesson, we explored various means that allow us to more effectively influence our fellows: family members, friends, coworkers, and all with whom we come into contact.

We learned of the importance of:

**1** Being motivated solely by our concern for our fellow

**2** Notifying the recipient that our motivation is concern for his or her welfare

**3** Not seeking to control our fellow

**4** Not judging or condemning our fellow for his or her actions

**5** Not having the conversation when either party is in an agitated state

**6** A private setting

**7** Soft and gentle demeanor, tone, and word content

**8** Speaking to the recipient's inherent goodness and infinite potential

*(Cont. on next page)*

Refer back to your responses to Exercise 2 (p. 121). Which of these skills can you apply to increase your influence?

In your family life:

In your business or social life:

In society at large:

## KEY POINTS

**1** The Hebrew word for communication is related to the word that means to lead and influence. This informs us that (a) a leader influences by way of words, and (b) the purpose of words is to influence.

**2** According to the Torah, everyone is responsible for their fellows' spiritual and moral welfare. Our collective mutual responsibility draws from our spiritual interconnectedness and our joint stake in the destiny of Creation.

**3** We all are capable of influencing others, regardless of our status or position. In fact, "average people" and their frank communications have a unique ability to exert influence.

**4** Any attempt to influence another must derive solely from genuine concern for our fellow. If we attempt to influence because the other's behavior or character bothers us, reflects badly on us, or rouses our moral indignation, it will not yield real and lasting results.

**5** The masculine mode of influence imposes and conquers. The feminine mode of influence cultivates and nurtures, and thus garners truer outcomes.

**6** When we see something unseemly in another person, we must discharge our obligation to help the other, but we must avoid making moral judgments, which engenders defensiveness.

**7** Attempting to influence a person while he or she is in an emotionally explosive state leads to more conflict and can exacerbate the issue.

**8** A most effective way to offer critique is to tell people how great they are and how what they are doing is unbefitting someone of their stature.

# Additional Readings

## A PEACE OF (MY) MIND

BY DAVID LAZERSON

"Now listen up," Reuven said, clearly annoyed. "You're heading for nothing but trouble. You'd better stop before it's too late. I wish you'd listen to my advice, Ari! I'm getting tired of always trying to tell you, but talking to you is like talking to the dang wall!"

Ari (the name has been deliberately changed here) had probably heard similar words a hundred times before. He was a young man of sixteen in my alternative high school program, Beth Rafael, in Miami. My program was nicknamed "Laz's Last Stand." They either made it in my program or ended up in rehab . . . or behind bars. Most, thank G-d, graduated from my non-graded program, got their high school diploma, and have moved on to lead positive, productive lives.

Ari was a great athlete, full of life and personality, but he had some rough experiences in regular school. He was close to the record, having been kicked out of more than ten schools in the past six years. Unsuccessful in his close-knit community, he viewed himself as an outcast, and had turned to the streets for acceptance. Reuven, a fellow classmate, was trying to offer some words of advice. Ari, it seems, had once again been out all night long doing who-knows-what.

**DAVID LAZERSON, PHD**

David Lazerson, fondly known as Dr. Laz, is world renowned for his innovative educational approach. He has received numerous awards for his accomplishments, including being named the 1981 Teacher of the Year in New York State. In 2008, Dr. Laz was inducted into the National Teachers Hall of Fame. As a race-relations specialist, he was called upon to liaise between the African American and Jewish communities after the Crown Heights riots. Dr. Laz is also a musician and has authored four books, including the best-selling *Skullcaps 'n Switchblades* (1987), which chronicles his time as a special education teacher in an inner city high school in Buffalo, NY.

He showed up mid-morning and laid his weary head upon the table.

"You don't know how good you got it here," Reuven continued. "But even this opportunity you're gonna blow just like all the others! You're gonna get locked up, bro . . . if you live long enough."

With that, Reuven slammed his fist on the table, but Ari was either fast asleep or simply chose to ignore the commotion.

I put my hand out and motioned for Reuven to lay off.

"Look," I whispered to Reuven, "talk to him when he wakes up. But I think maybe we should try a different approach."

He shot me a glance of disbelief and remarked, "He's gonna kill himself the way he's going! Someone's gotta do something!"

"Agreed," I responded. "Wholeheartedly. But has this approach ever worked for him? That's what he's been hearing, probably from everyone who knows him, for the past two, three years straight."

"So, what then? We should sit back, do nothing . . . and watch him slowly kill himself?"

"No. I'm just saying maybe there's a better way to reach him."

I promised Reuven that we'd discuss things together and try to come up with some strategies that might work. But there was this uncomfortable feeling, something that always bugged me but that I never quite verbalized. And yet, every so often, it would come bubbling up to the surface, like it was waiting to be validated, to be dealt with.

Then I had an epiphany and realized that all those thoughts of "doubt" were there for a solid reason. I had it all wrong—and, to a certain extent, we've all missed the boat here. Yes, I know that sounds like a mighty bold statement, but allow me to explain what's been bothering me all these years.

I refer to that tricky and very sensitive notion of setting the other guy straight, a.k.a. "reading someone the good ol' riot act." You know the one, this murky gray area of us knowing what's really proper (or thinking that we do), and putting our friends, family members, and even the "Joe Shmoes" we don't know so well, in line. It's the one that some folks have made their special mission—rebuking your fellow human being.

This is a mighty sensitive area that, at best, requires "kid glove" treatment and some real thoughtful, deliberate actions—not rash, emotional responses. I speak from some experience, having raised seven children (now all adults on their own). I've also been working with alienated teens and individuals with special needs for more than thirty years. Not that I have any definitive answers per se, except that I know that when it comes to the art of rebuking, I usually keep a very low profile. Others, it seems, have given this equal footing and rank it right up there with the "Ten Big Ones." Chabad philosophy stresses the angle that we have to help each other out on all levels. But it also teaches us that when it comes to spiritual growth, the real work, the hard work, starts with the "man in the mirror"—with ourselves first.

What's bugged me all these years is that the Torah uses a double-whammy expression to convey this message of rebuking others. It says rather bluntly, *"hoche'ach tochiach"*—which is usually translated as "you should surely rebuke": not just one word indicating "rebuke," but two Hebrew words to really get out there and give 'em the ol' what-for! Knowing what we do about human nature, I ask you a question. Do we really need a double expression from the One Above telling us to rebuke someone? Was G-d Almighty worried that we might not get in there and tell somebody, "Hey, you're messing up, and I know better—I know what's best for you!" Wouldn't it have been enough for it to say in the Torah just the one Hebrew word *tochiach*?

There are those who seem to thrive on putting others in line, of telling them what to do and what not do, and getting some sort of holier-than-thou satisfaction of putting them in their place. They've become the "rebukers," the crusaders to save us all . . . from ourselves!

It did help to study Tanya and listen to the deep words of the Alter Rebbe, the first Chabad Rebbe, on this double expression of rebuke. The Alter Rebbe stresses the latter part of that verse where it says you should surely rebuke *et amitecha*—the "one that is with you." In other words, only those with whom you are very close, the Alter Rebbe explains in the 32nd chapter of Tanya, should you rebuke. Interesting that the number thirty-two in Hebrew corresponds to the word *lev*, which means "heart." Furthermore, he writes, it has to be done with love and compassion. Let's face it here, folks. No one enjoys being put in his or her place. Nobody relishes the experience of being on the receiving end of a personal "dis." We usually accept this sort of stuff only from a loved one. A stranger telling us off doesn't sit too well and, in fact, often leads to the opposite desired effect. We tell the guy to take a long walk off a short pier.

Change doesn't come easy, and changing harmful or negative behaviors is tricky business—and often a long, uphill battle. The Alter Rebbe tells us that here it just might work if, in fact, someone who's close to the guy messing up does it. The rebukee, if you will, knows that the rebuker is a close friend or family member and has his or her best interest at heart.

Upon further research, I discovered that this word *"hoche'ach"* is used twice in the Torah portion of Chayei Sarah. Both are in the episode of Eliezer, Abraham's servant, being sent on a mission to find a wife for Isaac, Abraham's son.

It's quite a mission, and Eliezer, with Abraham's personal instructions and blessing, succeeds big-time. Standing near a watering hole at the edge of town, Eliezer puts this wheel into play and calls out to the "G-d of Abraham," asking for some tell-tale signs to know who is the right pick for Isaac. He's basically looking for someone who is a *mentch*, who shows kindness—even to a stranger.

If she offers me water to drink, Eliezer stipulates, and also offers to give water to my camels, then this is the one that *"hochachta"* for Isaac. Seems like a mighty strange word to use here. It's the very same root as the word for "rebuke." The foremost biblical commentator Rashi picks up on this unusual expression here and says that it actually means *"berarta"*—"You chose."

My cerebral cortex went in high gear. *B'reirah* in Hebrew means "to choose," "to select," and "to clarify." Maybe that double expression of "rebuke, rebuke" is mistranslated? Perhaps it also means more to clarify than to simply rebuke? The act of choosing and selecting is part and parcel of the act of clarifying. It's a matter of shedding some light on the options and selecting the best possible choice. And, sure enough, when the same word is used twenty-nine verses later, Rashi explains that it means "to clarify, to inform—and so too for every expression of the word *hochachah* in the Torah." Whereas all these outdated translations put in print for the double expression, "You shall surely rebuke!" Rashi is telling us that it really should read, "You shall surely clarify."

It's no small difference here. It's a difference of night and day. Both may try to get the person to "see the light," but one does it with a hammer, which has little chance of success, while the other does it with love, compassion and some common sense.

Furthermore, it's not a matter of coming across as holier-than-thou. It's not even coming from a "religious" perspective of "saving" this lowlife and getting another notch on the belt. It's simply a matter of shedding some light on the subject and helping the person in need get things straight—to see with more clarity. Then, and only then, is he or she in the proper position to decide, to choose which direction to go. Our job, then, Rashi points out, is not to rebuke but to illuminate! Not to give 'em a piece of our minds, but to offer them peace of mind.

Let's go back to the situation with Ari, and more specifically, how Reuven and I decided to handle things. It was a plan taken right out of Rashi's sage interpretation and advice. First, I gave Reuven the "green light" to speak with Ari. Sometimes, more often than not, teenagers listen to a friend more than a teacher. I told Reuven that words of rebuke, the ol' fire & brimstone routine, always fell on deaf ears, and thus, a new strategy was warranted. "Ari doesn't respond to that. Why not try a total unemotional vibe. Put out the consequences of his behaviors. Spell it out. Maybe, just maybe, he'll make some better choices. But in any case, I'd wait till he wakes up and has a good meal under his belt first."

It wasn't until a few days later that Reuven caught up with Ari. I couldn't help eavesdrop from the opposite corner of the room as the conversation took a different turn.

"Ari," he started. "Let's analyze the situation here. Things are good now 'cuz business is rolling. But eventually you're gonna get busted. It's just a matter of time. If you stop now, you'll make less money—at least for now, until things pick up in a proper and legal way—but you'll have a clean slate. If you carry on this way, you're probably looking at ten years minimum jail time, maybe more."

Ari tuned in because Reuven wasn't laying any guilt trip or holier-than-thou number on him. He simply put the cards on the table.

"One path might be tougher at first," Reuven continued, "but you won't have to worry about jail time or messing up your life. The other is great for now, you're riding high, but sooner or later the bubble is gonna burst. Think how it'll be then. For your friends and family. For you!"

I was amazed when Reuven suggested that they write down the choices, the pros and cons with all the consequences, on paper. Maybe, just maybe, I thought to myself, with the situation all spelled out and clarified, along with the concern and the friendship of a loving friend, Ari will make better choices.

Rashi is telling us that words of rebuke do very little to change the situation. Clarification, on the other hand, places the onus of choice on the person involved, without the guilt, and free of any rebuker's ego.

Torah is often compared to light. In this regard, the deeper we look into the Torah, the clearer and sweeter things become. Thanks, Rashi. I owe you one. And maybe we all do.

Reprinted with permission of the author

# HOW TO GIVE GOOD ADVICE

BY ROCHEL HOLZKENNER

A doctor and a lawyer were at a cocktail party, when the doctor was approached by a man who asked [for] advice on how to handle his ulcer. The doctor mumbled some medical advice, then turned to the lawyer and remarked, "I never know how to handle the situation when I'm asked for medical advice during a social function. Is it acceptable to send a bill for such advice?" The lawyer replied that it was certainly acceptable to do so.

The next day, the doctor received an invoice from the lawyer: $200 due for legal consultation.

*"Before the blind, do not put a stumbling block"*—Leviticus 19:14.

What are the everyday implications of the Torah's cautionary remark about sensitivity towards a blind man?

Here are some that come immediately to my mind:

- Not discriminating against people who are handicapped.
- Not exploiting people when they are vulnerable.
- Not setting out alcohol in front of a recovering alcoholic.
- Taking responsibility for other people's spiritual wellbeing, and not tempting them to sin.

Rashi, the Torah's foremost commentator, says that I'm wrong about what's being implied here. Personal liability is a topic that's already been laid out in the Torah in graphic detail; by now it's obvious that G-d doesn't let us hurt people who are at a disadvantage. In fact, we also can't hurt people who are not disadvantaged, and we must make restitution even if damage was done unintentionally.

So, Rashi wants to know, what's the new mitzvah that G-d is teaching us here?

He quotes the Talmud:

> *Someone who is blind in the matter at hand, you should not give advice which is unsuitable for him. Don't say, "Sell your field and buy a donkey," while you [plan on] setting him up and taking [the field] from him.*

The Torah is saying: Don't give someone dishonest advice. Not necessarily bad advice, just dishonest.

Let's look at the example: "Sell your field and buy a donkey." Not necessarily bad advice. In some cases, a donkey can be more valuable than a field; it works hard, produces offspring and is mobile. It may be a good idea to trade in the old field. But what's problematic about this advice is the hidden agenda; it's dishonest because it has the best interests of the advice-giver embedded within it. He wants that field.

The Torah is not telling us that we shouldn't hurt other people; that's obvious! It's not even telling us that we shouldn't give fictitious advice. The example about the donkey and field seems quite benign. And Rashi chooses this example since it's hard to discern whether the advice is good or not. But what's easy to discern is that it is good for the advice-giver.

So what the Torah is really telling us is this: When you give someone advice, don't let your personal agenda be a part of it. Even if you're not exploiting the other person with your advice. Even if your advice may be beneficial for him. If you stand to gain from it, then it's murky advice.

It's quite natural to look at any situation and search for personal benefit. But G-d says that that's not being a *mentch*. That's not an authentic way to communicate. "Love your neighbor as yourself!" When he asks you for advice, put yourself in his shoes, invest yourself in his dilemma as if it were yours. Then you can give some quality advice.[1]



**ROCHEL HOLZKENNER**

Rochel Holzkenner is a mother of four children and the codirector of Chabad of Las Olas, Florida, serving the community of young professionals.

**Endnotes**

1 Based on the teachings of the Lubavitcher Rebbe, Rabbi Menachem Mendel Schneerson, of righteous memory, recorded in *Likkutei Sichot*, vol. 27, pp. 141–148.

# *Acknowledgments*

*"The wise one: What is he saying?"*

—THE PASSOVER *HAGGADAH*

*An alternative way to translate these words is:*
*"The wise one: What is he? That which he is saying."*

—RABBI YOSEF YITSCHAK SCHNEERSOHN OF LUBAVITCH

It is the mission of the Rohr Jewish Learning Institute to plumb the infinite strata of Torah wisdom, to extract pearls of guidance and insight, and to then create courses that marry timeless truths to the relevant realities of modern society. We have covered medicine, law, psychology, finance, relationships, mysticism, and so many areas of life and belief. But there is one topic critical to them all: communication. If miscommunication is the mother of all misery and mayhem, then acquiring the skills of adequate and effective conversation opens our lives to individual and global cooperation and success.

Operating in an era of instant chat, speechless emojis, character-restricted Twittering, and wordless likes, JLI is pleased to present: *Communication: Its Art and Soul*. This course revisits the timeless art of verbal exchange and the compelling humanity of soul-to-soul communication. *Communication: Its Art and Soul* seamlessly combines divine wisdom with the latest scientific studies on the topic of communication.

We are grateful to the following individuals for helping shape this innovative course:

We extend our thanks to **Rabbi Naftali Silberberg** for his editorial oversight of this course. We extend our appreciation to **Rabbi Mordechai Dinerman**, who, along with Rabbi Naftali Silberberg, directs the JLI Curriculum Department and the Flagship editorial team; to **Rabbi Dr. Shmuel Klatzkin**, JLI's senior editor; and to **Rabbi Zalman Abraham**, who skillfully provides the vision for strategic branding and marketing of JLI course offerings.

We are grateful to **Rabbis Motty Schochet, Shmuel Super, Benyomin Walters,** and **Yosi Wolf**, who extensively researched the topics for this course, wrote and edited lesson drafts, and made substantial contributions to the course content. **Rabbis Yakov Gershon** and **Sholom Zirkind,** and **Leah Friedman** provided research assistance. **Zeldy Friedman** provided valuable editorial assistance throughout the production process.

The course was conceived and developed with guidance and direction from **Casey Skvorc, PhD,** and **Rus Devorah (Darcy F.) Wallen, LCSW, ACSW**. The JLI curriculum team was fortunate to draw on their vast erudition, experience, and expertise to develop a scholarly and relevant learning experience.

**Rabbi Yisroel Altein, Rabbi Sholom Raichik, Rabbi Yisrael Rice, Mrs. Michla Schanowitz** and **Rabbi Menashe Wolf**, members of the JLI Editorial Board, provided many useful suggestions that enhanced the course and ensured its suitability for a wide range of students.

**Rivki Mockin** and **Mushka Minsky** streamlined the curriculum process and ensured the smoothness and timeliness of the product, and **Chana Dechter,** JLI Flagship's administrator and project manager, contributed immeasurably to the production and professionalism of the entire project. **Mendel Schtroks** and **Shternie Morozow** designed the textbooks with taste, expertise, and patience. **Mushka Backman, Raizel Shurpin**, and **Chany Tauber** researched and selected the images for the textbook. **Mendel Sirota** directed the book publication and distribution. **Sarah Hinda Appelbaum, Chaya Super, Ya'akovah Weber,** and **Rachel Witty** enhanced the quality and professionalism of the course with their proofreading. **Baila Pruss** and **Mushka Druk** designed the aesthetically pleasing PowerPoints, and **Moshe Raskin** and **Getzy Raskin** produced the videos for this course. The video scripts were masterfully written by **Rabbi Yaakov Paley**.

We are immensely grateful for the encouragement of JLI's visionary chairman, and vice-chairman of *Merkos L'Inyonei Chinuch*—Lubavitch World Headquarters, **Rabbi Moshe Kotlarsky**. Rabbi Kotlarsky has been highly instrumental in building the infrastructure for the expansion of Chabad's international network, and is the architect of scores of initiatives and services to help Chabad representatives across the globe succeed in their mission. We are blessed to have the unwavering support of JLI's principal benefactor, **Mr. George Rohr**, who is fully invested in our work, continues to be instrumental in JLI's monumental growth and expansion, and is largely responsible for the Jewish renaissance that is being spearheaded by JLI and its affiliates across the globe.

The commitment and sage direction of JLI's dedicated Executive Board—**Rabbis Chaim Block, Hesh Epstein, Ronnie Fine, Yosef Gansburg, Shmuel Kaplan, Yisrael Rice**, and **Avrohom Sternberg**—and the countless hours they devote to the development of JLI, are what drive the vision, growth, and tremendous success of the organization.

Finally, JLI represents an incredible partnership of more than 1,400 *shluchim* and *shluchot* in more than one thousand locations across the globe, who contribute their time and talent to further Jewish adult education. We thank them for generously sharing feedback and making suggestions that steer JLI's development and growth. They are our most valuable critics and our most cherished contributors.

Inspired by the call of the **Lubavitcher Rebbe**, of righteous memory, it is the mandate of the Rohr JLI to **provide a community of learning** for all Jews throughout the world where they can participate in their precious heritage of Torah learning and experience its rewards. May this course succeed in fulfilling this sacred charge!

On behalf of the Rohr Jewish Learning Institute,

RABBI EFRAIM MINTZ
*Executive Director*

RABBI YISRAEL RICE
*Chairman, Editorial Board*

Torah Studies provides a rich and nuanced encounter with the weekly Torah reading.

Jewish teens forge their identity as they engage in Torah study, social interaction, and serious fun.

The Rosh Chodesh Society gathers Jewish women together once a month for intensive textual study.

TorahCafe.com provides an exclusive selection of top-rated Jewish educational videos.

Participants delve into our nation's past while exploring the Holy Land's relevance and meaning today.

This yearly event rejuvenates mind, body, and spirit with a powerful synthesis of Jewish learning and community.

Equips youths facing adulthood with education and resources to address youth mental health.

Select affiliates are invited to partner with peers and noted professionals, as leaders of innovation and excellence.

MyShiur courses are designed to assist students in developing the skills needed to study Talmud independently.

This rigorous fellowship program invites select college students to explore the fundamentals of Judaism.

A crash course that teaches adults to read Hebrew in just five sessions.

Machon Shmuel is an institute providing Torah research in the service of educators worldwide.

# The Rohr Jewish Learning Institute

AN AFFILIATE OF MERKOS L'INYONEI CHINUCH,
THE EDUCATIONAL ARM OF THE CHABAD-LUBAVITCH MOVEMENT
832 EASTERN PARKWAY, BROOKLYN, NY 11213

# The Jewish Learning Multiplex

*Brought to you by the Rohr Jewish Learning Institute*

In fulfillment of the mandate of the Lubavitcher Rebbe, of blessed memory, whose leadership guides every step of our work, the mission of the Rohr Jewish Learning Institute is to transform Jewish life and the greater community through the study of Torah, connecting each Jew to our shared heritage of Jewish learning.

While our flagship program remains the cornerstone of our organization, JLI is proud to feature additional divisions catering to specific populations, in order to meet a wide array of educational needs.

THE ROHR JEWISH LEARNING INSTITUTE

A subsidiary of Merkos L'Inyonei Chinuch,
the adult educational arm of the Chabad-Lubavitch movement

Made in the USA
Middletown, DE
22 February 2023

25267085R00093